FINANCIAL SERVICES: THE NEW CORE RULES

Michael Blair, MA, LLM, Barrister

General Counsel, Securities and Investments Board

Chairman, Bar Association for Commerce, Finance and Industry

BLACKSTONE PRESS LIMITED

First published in Great Britain 1991 by Blackstone Press Limited,
9-15 Aldine Street, London W12 8AW. Telephone 081-740 1173

ISBN: 1 85431 072 0

British Library Cataloguing in Publication Data
A CIP catalogue record for this book is available from the British Library

Typeset by Style Photosetting Ltd, Mayfield, East Sussex
Printed by BPCC Wheatons Ltd, Exeter

FINANCIAL SERVICES: THE NEW CORE RULES

CONTENTS

FOREWORD

Michael Blair is uniquely qualified to write this guide to the Principles and Core Rules for the Conduct of Investment Business. He explains 'the essential spine of the UK regulatory system for the conduct of investment business' with characteristic clarity. This work will be essential reading for all who are concerned with the conduct of investment business whether as legal advisers, compliance officers, investment practitioners or members of the investing public. The Principles and Core Rules, as explained by Michael Blair, set out the essential standards of morality and sound practice for the City and the investment world generally.

P J Cresswell
London

PREFACE

Here is a short account of 'the essential spine of the UK regulatory system for the conduct of investment business'. This is the description given in January 1991 by the Securities and Investments Board (SIB) to the Statements of Principle and the Core Conduct of Business Rules. Account is also taken in this book of the five core rules for financial supervision.

The principles came into effect in April 1990 and set out at high level the standards expected of all those carrying on investment business in the United Kingdom.

The financial supervision core rules came into effect in August 1990 and set out at high level the central themes relevant to capital adequacy and prudential supervision. These rules apply to most members of self-regulating organisations (SROs), but not, for example, to life offices.

The Core Conduct of Business Rules state in compressed and straightforward form the essence of conduct of business regulation, concentrating on the standards required in relation to private investors in particular. These rules will apply to members of SROs, but not until further commencement orders are made. There is a glossary to help in the interpretation of these rules.

This book therefore deals with a new subject that is partly already in force, and partly waiting to come into force.

Preface

I am grateful to colleagues and friends whose advice and encouragement has been of great help. I have written in my capacity as a private individual, and must not be taken to be expressing the views of the SIB.

Michael Blair
3 Gray's Inn Place
London WC1R 5EA

PART A THE PRINCIPLES

CHAPTER 1

INTRODUCTION

[1] The Financial Services Act 1986 brought in a new sophisticated system of regulation of investment business in the United Kingdom. This, in essence, was self regulation (or 'practitioner-based' regulation) in a statutory context. It evolved over the period from 1982 as an amalgam of what was seen as the best of the United Kingdom practice with an admixture of the United States experience stemming from 1934. It conferred strong new powers on the relevant regulators, which have since proved successful in practice. It caused there to be set up an industry-financed compensation scheme for private investors on a broadly comprehensive basis. A concomitant of the concept of self regulation was the financing arrangements: the taxpayer was not involved in the system, which was to be and is paid for by the participants and, through them, by the investors themselves.

[2] These benefits have been generally welcomed, though in some other respects the Financial Services Act 1986 has not been the most popular or generally praised piece of United Kingdom legislation. Three particular aspects of the legislation have proved a source of intermittent and sometimes sustained criticism.

[3] The first of these was the cost of the transition and of increased activity by firms in terms of compliance. Some of this was unavoidable, but many critics believed that cost was being needlessly caused

on a continuing basis by the impact on the industry and hence on the investing public of the second and third aspects below.

[4] The second of these was the large number of bodies involved in the self-regulatory arrangements. This was a perhaps inevitable consequence of the approach of practitioner-based regulation. It produced a certain amount of overlapping memberships and functions and, in consequence, a need for:

(a) multiple and variegated compliance within firms and groups;

(b) multiple and variegated systems of protection for investors, leading to complexities for them, and for those concerned in giving them advice, and

(c) orderly coordination and effective cooperation between the different regulatory bodies.

This problem has been and continues to be addressed. A step of major significance was the decision of two of the five self-regulating organisations (SROs) to merge on 1 April 1991 to form the Securities and Futures Authority. This produces a more rational and, it is expected, will produce a more economical structure. The high level of unification in rule making to be discussed in this book has also been a further contribution towards reducing variegation.

[5] The third major criticism, which is the most relevant of the three for this book, was the form and sheer bulk of the initial rule books prepared for the regulatory system in 1986-88. These turned out to have, or have had, four weaknesses; they were generally seen as

(a) too long, too detailed, and too prescriptive;

(b) not sufficiently integrated in practice (each had different wording from the next, different conceptual frameworks and different content, not only in areas of justifiable diversity, but elsewhere);

(c) in terms of content, not distinguishing adequately between the protection properly required for the private customer and that less intrusive amount required for institutional business;

(d) drafted in a convoluted and complex format, which made them rather difficult to understand and comply with, except in the case of trained and experienced lawyers.

[6] Relatively soon after commencement, therefore, calls were made for the system to be refashioned and simplified with a view to increasing the degree of comprehensibility and, accordingly, the amount of compliance. The Securities and Investments Board (SIB), by then under a new Chairman, took up this challenge, and produced a revised and more straightforward set of conduct of business rules. This appeared in late 1988, but was destined to remain forever a draft.

[7] The reactions to that draft, favourable in large measure, led to further discussions and thought, the end result of which was a suggestion to the Government that the process of simplification and integration could be given further impetus by some relatively modest legislative change to the Financial Services Act 1986. The main purposc of that reform was to give to the SIB a power to state essential or central requirements, on a unified basis, leaving it to the other regulatory bodies to create for themselves the supporting detail which they might find desirable.

[8] To this could be added that the test of equivalence was seen as falling short of the ideal. This was the mechanism through which Parliament, and the SIB, could be assured that the rule books of the recognised bodies delivered equivalent protection for investors to that put forward by the SIB itself and approved for the purpose of the Financial Services Act 1986 by Parliament. Changes to produce a more workable arrangement, based on adequacy rather than equivalence, were therefore also put forward at this stage.

[9] The combination of these two changes was intended to be that the SIB would concern itself with higher level requirements and not with fine detail except in so far as that was unavoidable.

[10] Those changes were carried into the Bill for the Companies Act 1989 in the spring and summer of 1989, thereby enabling the new arrangements contemplated to proceed. Since then, a great deal of effort has been put by practitioners, regulators and other interested commentators into the process of revision under the new framework, and this book seeks to give an account of the resulting simplified

approach. It is offered at the point at which the main contribution from the SIB to the process has been delivered, and in advance of the further contribution, the so-called 'third tier', now being worked upon by the relevant recognised bodies.

[11] The remainder of Part A discusses the investment business principles, the new, very high level, guiding lights. These have been in force since April 1990, and have since been a source of some interest in international discussions on the investment industry.

[12] At annex 5 is a set of conduct of business principles devised by the International Organisation of Securities Commissions (IOSCO), and adopted by it at its conference in Santiago, Chile in late 1990. The similarity between these international principles and those earlier adopted in the United Kingdom is noteworthy.[1]

[13] It now seems likely that something recognisably similar will be included in the forthcoming Investment Services Directive of the European Community. This would provide general harmony of orientation in the Community context on matters of a prudential nature (such as capital, financial supervision, client assets and compensation) and on matters relating to the conduct of investment business (diligence, disclosure, market integrity etc.).[2]

NOTES

[1] The IOSCO Conduct of Business Principles of December 1990 are seven in number, compared with the SIB's principles of March 1990 which number 10. One of the SIB principles (Principle 7 Customer assets) finds no place in the IOSCO set, since this subject is regarded in many overseas jurisdictions, and to some extent in the United Kingdom, as distinct from conduct of business and related more to issues of prudential supervision.

The remaining nine are all reflected in the IOSCO principles, with a broad comparison being as follows:

IOSCO	SIB
1. Honesty and fairness	1. Integrity (and principle 3 Market practice)
2. Diligence	2. Skill, care and diligence (and principle 3 Market practice)
3. Capabilities	8. Financial resources and 9. Internal organisation
4. Information about customers	4. Information about customers
5. Information for customers	5. Information for customers
6. Conflicts of interest	6. Conflicts of interest
7. Compliance	10. Relations with regulators (and principle 9 Internal organisation)

[2] The Investment Services Directive is still in draft, but is expected to be completed in time to give the Member States an adequate period to implement it before 1 January 1993.

CHAPTER 2

THE INDIVIDUAL PRINCIPLES

[1] This chapter contains a description of the content of the 10 principles, taken one by one. Chapter 3 then deals with the legal setting for the principles, including their status, application and enforcement.

Principle 1 Integrity

A firm should observe high standards of integrity and fair dealing.

[2] This principle and principle 2 (skill, care and diligence) are, in a sense, 'arch' principles, or overarching principles, covering in general terms all the material in the remaining eight. At the highest level of generality, these two are specifically drawn from the language of the Financial Services Act 1986 itself.[1]

[3] Principle 1 requires integrity and fair dealing. Included in integrity are the concepts of honesty, of straightforwardness and of honourable conduct. Included in fair dealing is the fundamental legal concept of fairness, which is easily recognised but hard to define. At bottom, fairness involves an approach to business based on two factors, rationality and balance. Rationality is relevant in part because of the inherent need that what is fair should be seen to be

rational; and in part because what was fair yesterday may not be fair today and the process of change must be achieved in a sensible way. The element of balance involves, first, the recognition of the existence of a balance between the interests of different customers, or between the interests of one or more customers and that of the firm; and, second, an obligation to conduct oneself in such a way as to ensure that the balance is reasonably held between those various interests.

[4] How far the content of the law on equitable conduct is imported by fair dealing is not clear: it seems likely that some at least of the various maxims of the English law of equity are closely relevant, including the notion that 'equality is equity'. On the other hand, others appear strictly foreign to the analysis. The 'clean hands' doctrine, for instance, implies, and derives from, a system of law which imposes rights and obligations in a general way; the doctrine then denies an equitable remedy to someone who is in breach of his own obligations. How far this doctrine is relevant to a system of principles which are capable of operating in a one sided way (in that they impose obligations on authorised persons and not on their (unauthorised) customers) remains to be seen.

[5] In the cases of integrity and of fair dealing alike the obligation is not an absolute one, but one based on high standards. This phrase is reproduced in principle 3 (high standards of market conduct) but not in any of the other eight: principle 2, by contrast, uses the concept of 'due' skill care and diligence. 'High standards' imports some judgmental discretion, while at the same time making it clear that the principles expect those governed by them to strive for improvement.

[6] Where another of the principles appears directly in point, the high standards expected by principle 1 will not require conduct to a standard more exacting than that in the detailed principle. It may help to illustrate this in relation to conflict of interest. Principle 6 offers to firms two different ways of proceeding. One of these is to avoid any conflict, and the other is to manage the conflict ('ensure fair treatment to all its customers by disclosure, internal rules of confidentiality, declining to act or otherwise'). Where there is that degree of detail in principle 6 overall, the requirement to observe high standards of fair dealing in principle 1 does not require firms to opt for the more rigorous of those two strategies. They might be required to opt in that way, if there was no other course open that ensured fair

treatment; but that would be a decision driven by the obligation of fair treatment in principle 6 and not that of fair dealing in principle 1.

[7] The element of discretion may also be of relevance in relation to disclosure. A false statement is *prima facie* a breach of a duty to observe high standards of integrity, at any rate where the intention to deceive is proved, or where the honesty of the mistake is not established. What, however, of the suggestion by a client that there was a lack of integrity in not correcting a statement that had become false through the operation of time? High standards of integrity require correction where there is an outlying duty (in contract or by operation of law) or established practice of correction.

[8] Lastly what will be made of the proposition that what may appear to the lawyers to be a failure to observe high standards of integrity and fair dealing is in fact common practice in the City of London, or in the market or business community concerned? This is best considered in the context of principle 3 below.

Principle 2 Skill, care and diligence

A firm should act with due skill, care and diligence.

[9] As noted in the context of principle 1, this principle is an overarching principle, covering much of what follows in the remaining principles. In requiring skilled, careful and attentive conduct wherever that is due, it does not create much, if any, new law. It appears to require the generally accepted standards of the general law, particularly those in the tort, or delict, known as negligence. There is, however, a change in terms of remedy, to be discussed in chapter 3, rather as has happened in relation to solicitors in England and Wales following the enactment in 1985 of new provisions providing disciplinary obligations in respect of 'shoddy work'.

[10] Since 1989, the financial community and its regulators have become increasingly concerned with the standards of competence of those engaged in the industry. A report, 'Training and Competence in the Financial Services Industry' by Dr Oonagh McDonald (the former Labour Member of Parliament and member of the Opposi-

tion front bench) has recommended, over a five-year time-scale, the introduction of more exacting standards of professionalism in the financial services industry.[2] It seems likely that introduction of these new measures will be reinforced by principle 2. If the level of skill required for those entering into the industry is effectively raised, public expectation as to what is due will also rise; and it will not look impressive to a disciplinary tribunal if a firm argues that the persons concerned with a particular alleged shortcoming had all entered the industry before the new standard and therefore did not have a duty to be as skilful as the newcomers.

Principle 3 Market practice

A firm should observe high standards of market conduct. It should also, to the extent endorsed for the purpose of this principle, comply with any code or standard as in force from time to time and as it applies to the firm either according to its terms or by rulings made under it.

[11] This principle is two headed, with one head in each of the two sentences. The first head, 'high standards of market conduct', virtually makes a third 'arch' principle to set alongside principles 1 and 2. The second head, not yet in force for reasons to be explained below, will require in due course compliance with certain external codes or standards.

[12] There are two issues relating to that part of the principle concerned with market conduct: what does it add to principles 1 and 2, and what, if anything, does it take away? In terms of adding to the principles, the duty to observe high standards of market conduct means that the special standards of conduct in particular markets rank as relevant in their own right to those who practise in those markets. This may be significant, for instance, for those who operate in the stock or gilts markets, or on commodities exchanges.

[13] It is not stated whether a special sector of the financial services industry, not involving an exchange as such, can nevertheless be a market for this purpose, but the context strongly suggests that it can be so regarded. The extent to which market functions (in the sense of

bringing together buyers and sellers) are obtainable only within the intermediation of a formal exchange varies enormously within the industry, and the balance between on- and off-exchange transactions is regulated in different ways in different sectors.[3] There is, however, a market wherever there is a place, mechanism or other opportunity for buyers and sellers to deal with each other, directly or indirectly.

[14] A second addition to principles 1 and 2 is caused by the fact that principle 3 requires firms to behave with high standards to the markets themselves, and principle 3 has a systemic focus in that sense. Irrespective of integrity and fair dealing towards a customer or counterparty, a firm must acknowledge the needs of the market.[4] Failure to meet obligations under the rules of exchanges and thereby setting up risks for other parties and for the relevant clearing house could therefore be regarded as a breach of this principle, and so the consequential closing out of the transaction and action at law for recovery of the sum would not be the only sanctions. Although the principles do not of themselves bind recognised investment exchanges or the members of such exchanges, they are of course applicable to those members in their capacity as authorised persons.[5]

[15] What, if anything, does principle 3 take away from principle 1? Paragraph 6 above concluded that principle 1 would not require a standard more exacting than that required by the more detailed principles, such as principle 6. While that approach seems, on the face of it, applicable to the detailed second half of principle 3, what of the general obligation of high standards of market conduct itself? In particular, is it likely that a market participant will be able to say: 'But principle 1 cannot expect me to behave to a standard more exacting than that prevailing among practitioners in this market?'[6] That this is a real question can be seen from the concern of late expressed by some in the context of section 47 (misleading statements and practices) of the Financial Services Act 1986 and from certain cases currently being investigated or prosecuted. The worry has been that some long standing and hitherto genuinely accepted practices in the securities industry and in the world of corporate finance may now be regarded as unlawful. It is suggested that the answer, in relation to principle 1, is that the requirement of observance of high standards of market practice will not of itself provide a defence to an otherwise credible allegation of lack of integrity. On the other hand, compliance with an applicable detailed principle (e.g. principle 5 (information for

customers)) may provide a defence to allegations of breach of principle 1,[7] and the same will almost certainly be true, in practice if not also as a matter of law, of compliance with an applicable core rule such as core rule 29 (stabilisation of securities) or core rule 10 (customers' understanding of risk) as regards any relevant disclosures.

[16] The second part of principle 3 relates to endorsement of codes or standards. Specifically enabled by the Financial Services Act 1986, section 47A(2), this permits outlying informal obligations to be incorporated into the principle, so that an investment firm would then, on pain of regulatory sanctions, be required to observe the relevant code at least in the context of its investment business. The codes principally regarded as relevant for this purpose (at the time of the legislation and subsequent consultation documents) have been:

(a) the City Code on Takeovers and Mergers (including the Rules Governing Substantial Acquisitions of Shares)

(b) the Bank of England's so-called London Code, which relates to wholesale markets in gilts, foreign exchange and bullion, and is included in the Bank's 'Grey Book', and

(c) the Oil Markets Code, applicable to so-called oil market participants, that is authorised firms which operate in the oil futures markets, particularly the Brent oil market.

[17] At present the second half of the principle is inoperative, because the 'endorsement' in question requires a formal act on the part of the SIB.

[18] For some time the SIB has had in mind the desirability of issuing an instrument of endorsement of codes, and has been having discussions with the various recognised bodies in this respect. It is anticipated that the instrument of endorsement would make provision for two points of legal interest specifically uncovered by section 47A. These are:

(a) the power of a statement of principle to include compliance with a code or standard issued by another person as for the time being in force; and

(b) the power of a statement of principle to allow for the exercise of discretion by any person pursuant to any such code or standard.

[19] Both of these are specifically referred to in section 47A(2) (and in principle 3 itself) and, in general terms, Parliament envisaged that the statement of principle could involve 'rolling incorporation', and the incorporation of an obligation to obey decisions made (typically by the Takeover Panel) pursuant to a code. These decisions could relate to the substance of past cases before the person exercising discretion, or to modification or dispensing with requirements of the code in relation to current cases.

Principle 4 Information about customers

A firm should seek from customers it advises or for whom it exercises discretion any information about their circumstances and investment objectives which might reasonably be expected to be relevant in enabling it to fulfil its responsibilities to them.

[20] This is known as the 'know your customer' principle. It arises in two circumstances:

(a) where the firm is advising the customer, and

(b) where the firm exercises discretion for a customer,

but not in any other cases. Thus so-called 'execution only' deals are excluded, as are any other non-customer counterparties. In this way the principle seeks to put in one (excluded) category persons to whom no fiduciary duty is owed, and persons the fiduciary duty towards whom can be discharged without seeking information from them about their circumstances and objectives. In another (protected) category are the so-called advisory and discretionary customers towards whom, as will be seen below, certain other specific duties are contained in the core rules.[8] It should be noted that there is no core rule specifically on 'know your customer': principle 4, unusually among the principles, leads to no more detailed outworking in the core rules except for a glancing reference in core rule 16(1) (suitability). The rationale for this is twofold. First, this aspect of a firm's duty can best be expressed in reasonably general terms, is unlikely to need further sanctions on its own by way of civil enforceability and is more easily enforced by the regulator by way of discipline than by the dissatisfied customer in the courts. Secondly, in cases where breach of the obligation to 'know your customer' causes loss or other adverse effect, there will almost certainly be a remedy under the core rules on suitability (16) and/or standards of advice on packaged products (17) and/or churning and switching (26).

[21] As to the information to be sought, the principle requires 'information about their circumstances and investment objectives which might reasonably be expected to be relevant in enabling it to fulfil its responsibilities' to the relevant customers. This reference to responsibilities, coupled with the stress on investment objectives, must be taken as relating back to the advisory and discretionary tasks and responsibilities arising there (including those arising under the core rules just mentioned). The information is to be sought from the customer, rather than about him. In the case of a customer who is a trustee, however, it will plainly relate to information about the trust's circumstances including the obligation which it has or may have towards individual beneficiaries.

[22] The obligation is to seek rather than necessarily to obtain the information. So, if the customer indicates an unwillingness to impart information, the investment firm will not be in breach of the principle: the principle itself does not prevent transactions from being carried out in such circumstances even though information relevant in enabling responsibilities to be fulfilled is absent.[9] In some circumstances, however, it can be envisaged that a firm might find it difficult to discharge its responsibilities without the requested information, and may prefer to decline the business and thus not be put at risk of breach of principle 4 or indeed other of its obligations to such a customer.

[23] In recent months, there has been a good deal of emphasis on the general question of money laundering. A draft Directive is in progress in the European Community in Brussels, and guidance has been prepared for banks and other businesses in the United Kingdom which might be expected to confront the problem of contaminated money. One of the topics being discussed in that context is one of

'know your customer', that is in the sense that the bank or other business should not take on the would-be customer without making some enquiry into the source of his money, at any rate where suspicions are aroused. This subject is not apt for inclusion under principle 4, not only because it is limited to the advisory and discretionary case, but also because the principle appears to be drafted as an obligation to the customer, rather than as an obligation to society at large. Questions of money laundering would accordingly fall to be dealt with, at the level of these principles, in the context of principle 1.

Principle 5 Information for customers

A firm should take reasonable steps to give a customer it advises, in a comprehensible and timely way, any information needed to enable him to make a balanced and informed decision. A firm should similarly be ready to provide a customer with a full and fair account of the fulfilment of its responsibilities to him.

[24] This is the principle about disclosure, and also about accountability. Like principle 3, it is double headed, each head being in a separate sentence. Like principle 4 it is, in the first of the two parts, directed at the firm's conduct towards some only of its customers: in this case however, the subset of customers is those whom the firm advises. Principle 5, on the other hand, is concerned with a narrower group of customers limited to those who are being advised and excluding those for whom the firm exercises discretion. The second part of principle 5 applies to all customers.

[25] The first part is a 'reasonable steps' provision, pivoting on what might be regarded as reasonable steps for the firm to take. Principle 4, by contrast, brings in the concept of reasonableness not as part of the steps taken by the firm (since the obligation it imposes is that of seeking information): but as part of the test of what might be regarded as relevant information. On either approach common law standards of reasonableness seem to be contemplated. So the first phrase of this first part of Principle 5 is on relatively narrow and familiar ground. The second phrase, however, contains four adjectives which together make the provision far reaching in its effect.

These four are:

comprehensible; timely;	}	in relation to manner of disclosure by the firm
balanced; informed	}	in relation to the decision (of the customer being advised) towards which the information supplied is leading.

[26] Much ink has been spilt, and much effort expended, in 1987-1990 on the vexed question of disclosure (generally), and (in particular) of disclosure to customers by independent financial advisers and by product company agents of relevant information about packaged products. Ministers have recently (December 1990) expressed dissatisfaction with the effect of the current rules on competition, and have called for fresh proposals to be introduced by the summer of 1992. Principle 5 has arrived on the scene, therefore, between the first and the second phases of this debate. It is possible that it may make some contribution to that debate which has just been in part the subject of an issues paper by the SIB entitled 'Retail Regulation: issues for review' of April 1991. The information must be comprehensible, that is, not wrapped up in technical language or tucked away in a footnote; and it must be timely, that is it must be made available ('given') to the customer, not only rapidly and without quibbling, but at the moment which enables him to make a balanced and informed decision. Where a cancellation period of 14 days is offered pursuant to statute, timeliness must ensure that the information is available, at the latest, in time to enable the contract to be cancelled. If, however, further developments in marketing and regulatory requirements were to result in evolution in the meaning of timeliness, the result could be that information should be given to the customer (at least in cases where this is seen to be practicable in terms of technology and selling circumstances) in time to assist the customer with the initial decision.

[27] The other pair of adjectives, 'balanced' and 'informed', impose rather exacting standards, and need to be analysed in the context of the advisory customer's decision making. In essence, the decision making capability in such a case is divided between the investment firm and the customer. One is (or should be) the expert in the markets

and well informed about recent and anticipated trends: the other has not given up discretion to the firm, but has retained for himself the task of appraising the advice and taking the final decision. In practice, some of the customers will be more reliant than others on the investment firm's skill and knowledge. Some will themselves be expert, as in the case of the trustees of a major pension fund. Others, like the trustees of a deceased's estate, may have some knowledge of investment matters but may feel obliged, by the will and the general law as well as by their own limited experience, to seek investment advice; yet others will be virtually ignorant of the investments concerned and would be faced, perhaps on their own doorstep, by a representative about whose status as an adviser or as a salesman they may be somewhat unclear.

[28] In all cases, however, principle 5 expects that the information provided should be such as to enable the customer to make a balanced and informed decision. Though not expressly mentioned in principle, the two aspects of prime importance are 'information as to the nature of the investment and the financial implications of the transaction'. These are two aspects singled out by Parliament in this context, in the instructions it gave as to the context of the SIB's conduct of business provisions: see the Financial Services Act 1986, schedule 8, paragraph 7. It seems likely that the more the customer relies on the skill and judgment of the adviser, the more explanation will be needed. This need not however be in exhaustive detail: the risks of incomprehensibility and 'information overload' need to be assessed against the customer's need for adequate decision making material, with priority being given to the latter.

[29] Why 'balanced' as well as 'informed'? There are probably two answers to that question. First, a decision is balanced as well as informed if it is based on knowledge about the possible disadvantages as well as the advantages of a particular investment and gives each material fact its due weight. There is a correlation between the chance of profit and the risk of loss, and 'secure' investments, in an inflationary world, almost invariably involve some erosion of capital in real terms. Secondly a decision is balanced as well as informed if it is based on an adequate degree of information about how the proposed investment would fit into the overall pattern for the capital or savings of the customer.

[30] The second limb of principle 5 deals with accountability. The basic obligation is to be ready to provide a full and fair account of the fulfilment of the firm's responsibilities to the customer. This implies an orderly system of records of transactions[10] and a willingness to provide accountability on demand or on reasonable notice. The obligation extends beyond advisory customers to all customers, including the discretionary customer, and the execution only customer.[11] Obligations of some sort will be owed to any customer, however little he may have relied on the firm; for instance duties of best execution are normally owed even to an execution only customer.

[31] The account must be full and fair. Where therefore netting off of transactions to show a net position is fair in the circumstances (e.g. where the purpose of the report is to show current value) there may be no need to show the detail of the underlying transactions: but if the purpose of seeking the report was to verify the individual transactions as entered into historically, the process of netting to show the up-to-date position would be a short cut and neither full nor fair.

[32] It will be seen therefore that the second aspect of principle 5 is, in effect, 'customer driven'. The firm is ready to supply on request, and it is the customer who indicates what form the accountability is to take. It seems therefore that the word 'similarly' at the junction of the two separate obligations is without legal significance, and, in particular, does not import from the first limb the concept of reasonable steps or the limitation to customers who are being advised.

Principle 6 Conflicts of interest

A firm should either avoid any conflict of interest arising or, where conflicts arise, should ensure fair treatment to all its customers by disclosure, internal rules of confidentiality, declining to act, or otherwise. A firm should not unfairly place its interests above those of its customers and, where a properly informed customer would reasonably expect that the firm would place his interests above its own, the firm should live up to that expectation.

[33] This principle, on a highly complex subject, is the longest and at the same time the most complex of the 10. It is also unique among the principles in two ways; it contains three separate heads of obligation, more than any of the other nine, and it is the only principle to offer expressly a choice of methods of compliance, and indeed a choice at two levels. The complexity is due at least in part to the need to fashion basic and comprehensible rules relating to conflict of interest in the context of the UK securities markets as they have evolved in the run up to, and in the shadow of 'Big Bang' in 1986. The arrival of the so called 'integrated house' which has arms, or subdivisions of the same corporate entity, dealing with market making, with agency broking, with merchant banking and with other financial services activities means that the general subject of conflict of interest is made more intricate and at the same time more vital than in the earlier days of single capacity, and before ownership of brokers by banks was allowed.

[34] The first part of principle 6 offers to firms two ways of handling conflict of interest. The first option, perhaps more likely to be taken by professional firms such as solicitors[12] or accountants, is to avoid any conflict of interest arising. Prevention, on this footing, is better than cure. The second option is, put loosely, the successful management of the conflict. This is to be achieved by ensuring that there is fair treatment to all the firm's customers. The requirement for fair treatment arises both where there is a conflict between customer A and customer B, and where the conflict is between either (or both) of them and the firm itself.

[35] Where the firm selects management of conflict as its strategy, as will be appropriate with, for instance, integrated houses or with firms which deal as principal (with their own 'book') and as agent, it is presented with a further, tactical, choice. Under principle 6 fair treatment to customers is to be achieved:

(a) by disclosure;
(b) by internal rules of confidentiality;
(c) by declining to act, or;
(d) otherwise.

[36] 'Disclosure' of the existence of conflict may frequently be enough, though there will be cases where its nature and extent must

also be mentioned. If the customer knows that the firm has a stake in the matter, he will normally be able to judge whether that interest is likely to do him any harm. In some cases both interests may actually be working in the same direction, in which case there is no conflict. Where there is adequate competition, the opportunity which the customer has of taking his business elsewhere should normally be sufficient. In some cases disclosure will not be a practical option e.g. because it would reveal the firm's market making position or the plans of another customer. Another option may therefore have to be chosen.

[37] By 'internal rules of confidentiality' the principle refers to Chinese walls, as to which see core rule 36 below. There is specific provision in section 48(2)(h) of the Financial Services Act 1986 enabling rules (not, be it understood, principles) made by the SIB to provide defences against what might otherwise have been regarded as wrongful conduct pursuant to section 47 (misleading statements and practices) of that Act.

[38] 'Declining to act' is more far reaching than either of the first two choices offered. Indeed, it might frequently be regarded as a means of avoiding the conflict from arising in the first place, at any rate if the decision is taken promptly. The principle is not precise as to whether, in the event of a conflict of interest involving customer A and customer B, the firm should cease to act for both, or, if only for one, how it is to select the customer to be retained. Since, however, the context is that of managing conflict, it seems that retaining any one may be acceptable, the firm following its own perceived advantage in reaching the decision as between the customers.

[39] 'Otherwise' could involve other specially constructed methods. Putting the firm's own position temporarily into the discretionary management of another firm is one possible way,[13] though the firm would need to beware of the signal that such an unusual act might send to that other firm. Alternatively the core rules on allocation of bargains[14] may themselves be thought apt in a particular case to ensure that the customers are ensured fair treatment.

[40] It appears that, at the level of principles, the choice between the 'avoid' and 'manage' strategies, and, under 'manage', between the four offered tactical methods listed at paragraph 35 above, is a choice

for the firm. There should in general be no room for the argument, in the mouth of the customer, 'but I would have been better off had the firm avoided rather than managed' or 'the firm should have disclosed to me and not relied on Chinese walls'. The customer could, however, claim in an appropriate case that the method chosen had not been 'fair treatment'. The principle appears to be neutral as between the various choices, and does not establish a hierarchy between them, or even indicate that the firm must choose the strategy or tactical method that is most appropriate in the circumstances, so long as it achieves a fair result.

[41] The first part of the second sentence of principle 6 requires a firm not unfairly to place its own interests above those of its customers. Placing both interests level, and the limits on that, are dealt with in the second part (see paragraph 42 below). If therefore a firm proposes to put itself ahead of the customer it must ensure that this is fair. Cases where such priority would be fair will include, for instance, the charging of proper fees for services rendered or the existence of a spread between offer and bid prices.

[42] In a competition for priority between a firm and the customer, there will be occasions where the customer must come first. Indeed the Financial Services Act 1986 fully expected that there would be provision to that effect.[15] When, however, is this to be so? The answer given by the principle is 'whenever a properly informed customer would reasonably expect it'. This formulation appears to be fully objective: irrespective of the actual state of informedness of the particular customer, the question is based on the reasonable expectations of a properly informed customer. Such an expectation might arise because of general market practice, or a firm's settled and publicly known policy. It might also arise because of the particular course of events relating to the customer concerned, such as assurances by the salesman or investment manager concerned that the firm would always look after its customers first. Accordingly it seems that the hypothetical properly informed customer is a reasonable and properly informed customer in the actual customer's position. In this respect, it is possible to visualise circumstances where this reasonable person might differ in his expectation from the actual customer in his own actual circumstances, whether in favour of an accord of priority to the customer, or against.

Principle 7 Customer assets

Where a firm has control of or is otherwise responsible for assets belonging to a customer which it is required to safeguard, it should arrange proper protection for them, by way of segregation and identification of those assets or otherwise, in accordance with the responsibility it has accepted.

[43] This principle deals with proper protection of 'client money' and other assets belonging to customers, where either is entrusted to the firm. Under the Financial Services Act 1986, as it has evolved, the treatment of client money and of other assets belonging to customers has been somewhat fragmented. In general client money questions have been regulated by the SIB under its regulations made under section 55,[16] while customer assets matters have been left to be governed by the various sets of conduct of business rules made by the individual regulators. This variegation is not followed in principle 7, which seeks to provide a single proposition about client money and other assets alike.

[44] The principle applies wherever a firm 'has control of or is otherwise responsible' for assets which it is required to safeguard. A firm retains control or responsibility even where the assets are held to its order by a nominee company or other 'bare' trustee.[17] The important issue about applicability of principle 7 will therefore normally be whether the firm is 'required to safeguard' the assets. That requirement may come about by the working of the regulations on client money (for other assets core rule 32 (safeguarding of customer investments)) or by the relevant set of conduct of business rules; or it may be imposed by contract or by custom. Even if the actual assets are deposited by the firm with a bank, the firm must account properly for them. It also seems that the firm will remain responsible in some sense for assets even if they are held by a relevant clearing house in the form of margin[18] and so cease to be 'client money' in the ordinary way. Though it is questionable whether the firm is at that stage required to safeguard the actual assets, it is still required to act as the channel with the legal responsibility relating to that function and arguably must not permit those assets to be dissipated by an improper instruction to the clearing house, whether that instruction is induced by fraud within the firm or otherwise.

[45] The obligation is to arrange proper protection for the assets in accordance with the responsibility which the firm has accepted.[19] That 'acceptance' may of course be voluntary, as in the case of a contract, or obligatory, as in the case of applicable rules and regulations. The principle goes on, however, to offer the specific advantage of ensuring that the assets do not fall into the hands of the liquidator of the firm in the event of its insolvency, but are available to be recovered by the true owners at that point. This would normally be achieved, in the case of client money, by the use of the pooled trust set up under the SIB's client money regulations. The firm is established as the trustee (or in Scotland agent) of the money in the client money pool or pools and that money is segregated from the firm's own money by the use of client bank accounts with banks which acknowledge the legal segregation. Assuming proper accounting and no shortfall, the consequence on a default of the firm is that the money can readily be repaid. In the case of customer assets, the notice of identification may be even more important since segregation of physical assets as separate from those of the firm without identification customer by customer will not protect them as effectively in the case of a shortfall as if there is identification of the individual entitlements of different customers.

[46] The principle acknowledges, however, that the protection offered by segregation and identification may not always be appropriate. In the case of commodities, for instance, physical singling out of part of a bulk cargo may not be possible. In the case of the Personal Equity Plan, it may be unrealistically expensive to break down the individual holdings of each of the many plan holders. In the case of the more professional and experienced investors, the SIB's client money regulations already envisage that segregation may be waived by written agreement, on the hypothesis that such investors should be able to gauge whether the additional risk they carry themselves by opting out of segregation is outweighed by a reduction in the firm's dealing and managing costs.

Principle 8 Financial resources

A firm should ensure that it maintains adequate financial resources to meet its investment business commitments and to withstand the risks to which its business is subject.

[47] This principle deals in summary fashion with the complex and important subject of capital adequacy. It is specifically enabled by the reference in the Financial Services Act 1986, section 47A(1) to 'financial standing'. In this one respect the principles depart from the normal ambit of investment business and deal with the financial resources of the authorised firm taken as a whole, even if only part of its affairs is concerned with investment business. In doing so, principle 8 follows the prevailing philosophy in capital adequacy matters, i.e., that it is not possible to isolate the risks arising from particular activities carried on within the same entity. This problem is exacerbated where the entity is an unincorporated sole trader.

[48] Principle 8 also follows the prevailing philosophy in capital adequacy matters in another important respect. The obligation is one 'to ensure'. This imposes a strict standard, with no excuses (except, no doubt, *force majeure*) and no gloss by way of 'reasonable steps'. The importance, particularly from a systemic point of view, of a solid capital base for investment business firms has become increasingly apparent in recent years.

[49] The resources need to be adequate for two purposes; firstly for meeting the firm's investment business commitments, and secondly for withstanding the risks to which its business is subject. At the level of principles, therefore, firms are not specifically required to maintain financial resources to cover non-investment business commitments; but in the detailed (financial supervision) rules firms are required to take account of any such commitments.

[50] The primary focus in respect of commitments must be available liquid capital, or, at the least, capital that will be liquid by the time a future commitment matures. In relation to risks, however, the principle appears to envisage other forms of resource available to the firm in case of need, such as protection by way of insurance, whether on an individual or collective basis, and whether obtained voluntarily or as a regulatory requirement.

Principle 9 Internal organisation

A firm should organise and control its internal affairs in a responsible manner, keeping proper records, and where the firm employs staff or is responsible for the conduct of investment business by others, should have adequate arrangements to ensure that they are suitable, adequately trained and properly supervised and that it has well-defined compliance procedures.

[51] Although described as concerned with internal organisation, this principle is generally known as the 'compliance' principle, and is one of general importance in relation to regulation. Indeed, experience of the principles derived over the early months by regulators suggests that principles 1, 2 and 9 are those most commonly referred to in compliance and disciplinary reports.

[52] The ambit of this principle is best explained by means of a table:

Firms not employing staff	Firms employing staff	Firms responsible for the conduct of investment business by others
1 Organise and control internal affairs in a responsible manner 2 Keep proper records	3 As 1 4 As 2 5 Have adequate arrangements to ensure that staff are: (a) suitable (b) adequately trained (c) properly supervised 6 Have well-defined compliance procedures	7 As 1 8 As 2 9 Have adequate arrangements to ensure that those others are: (a) suitable (b) adequately trained (c) properly supervised 10 As 6

[53] Items 7-10 in the table, seen in this light, relate mainly though not exclusively to appointed representatives. These are persons, other than employees, who conduct investment business on the footing that the authorised person takes responsibility for their conduct.[20] They benefit from a special exemption if:

(a) the principal accepts responsibility in writing for their investment business;

(b) there is a contract between the principal and the appointed representative which limits the extent to which they may conduct such business with or for others (or at least enables the principal to impose such limits); and

(c) the business concerned is within the limits (mainly advice and arrangements) set out in the Financial Services Act 1986 section 44(3).

[54] In the early years of the UK system of regulation there have been some celebrated cases of difficulties over appointed representatives, particularly where the business concerned has been life insurance and the principal is a life office. Principle 9 makes it clear that the principal must have adequate arrangements for the purposes of item 9 of the table, and that the firm's compliance arrangements have to extend to cover these other individuals or corporate entities. This subject matter is taken much further by core rule 13 (see chapter 6).

Principle 10 Relations with regulators

A firm should deal with its regulator in an open and cooperative manner and keep the regulator promptly informed of anything concerning the firm which might reasonably be expected to be disclosed to it.

[55] The last of the 10 principles moves into new ground, in that the regulator appears in its own right for the first time. While the regulator has been concealed behind much of what has gone before (e.g. the regulatory requirements to safeguard assets in principle 7) it

now appears as a visible actor on the scene. The obligation is, first, to deal with the regulator in an open and cooperative manner, and, secondly, to keep it informed of anything concerning the firm which might reasonably be expected to be disclosed to it. The regulator is defined in the fourth paragraph of the Introduction (see annex 1) as the SIB or a self-regulating organisation or professional body which regulates the firm.[21] This means effectively an organisation or body recognised by the SIB for the purpose, and, in a case where both SIB and a regulator recognised by the SIB have a legitimate interest in the volunteering of information, the principle requires disclosure to both.

[56] The obligation to 'deal' in an open and cooperative manner is wide and unspecific. Refusal of consent to prearranged or unannounced compliance visits appears squarely within the prohibition, as is delay in dealing with correspondence or enquiries. Whether the principle covers the handling of complaints is more open to question: it seems likely, however, that a complaint in which the regulator is the avenue of communication, or one in the outcome of which it had expressed an interest, would be covered.

[57] As to the supply of information, there are two limiting factors which serve to keep an otherwise open-ended obligation within bounds. First, the information relates to the firm, rather than to a customer or competitor. Accordingly the principle leaves untouched the outlying law of breach of confidence, of legal professional privilege and of other legal or customary obligations to report (or immunities in respect of reporting) suspicious or criminal conduct. Secondly, the information has to be disclosed only if it concerns anything which might reasonably be expected to be disclosed to the regulator. This fully objective test of reasonableness is intended to make for efficiency in the supply of information and in action taken as a result and to resolve any difficulties which might otherwise have arisen about privilege or breach of confidence. Though it is always easier with hindsight to say that something should have been disclosed, the principle appears apt to require a supply of information late in the day if it was only then that the firm realised that the regulator might reasonably have expected to have learned of the problem. This may be particularly relevant in relation to emerging risks and commitments and to a moving capital position under principle 8: the individual sets of rules on financial resources make it plain that new and emerging risks etc. are to be reported to the

regulator even in advance of a monthly or quarterly financial statement.

NOTES

[1] See the Financial Services Act 1986, schedule 8, paragraphs 1A and 2.
[2] See the SIB's consultative paper No. 40 of May 1990.
[3] See for instance core rule 27.
[4] These two strands of obligation, to the customer and the market, underlie the section of the core rules on 'market integrity' and, in particular, the obligation in core rule 31 to report to the regulator specific transactions entered into off-exchange.
[5] In respect of the investment business which they do.
[6] See paragraph 8 above.
[7] But note that, in terms of pre-contractual disclosure, principle 5 applies only to customers who are being advised, and therefore cannot be said to have been complied with where the customer is not actually being advised, or where the person concerned is not a customer or potential customer.
[8] See for example, core rules 2 and 3. 'Advisory', in relation to a customer, conventionally means a customer who has been taken on the basis that he will receive advisory services. 'Discretionary' has a similar (conventional) meaning.
[9] The firm must, however, remember that core rule 16(1), if applicable, imposes duties on the basis of information of which the firm reasonably should be aware.
[10] See the discussion on principle 9 at paragraphs 52-4.
[11] The principles do not attract the meanings in the glossary to the Core Conduct of Business Rules. 'Customer' in the principles is therefore undefined except for paragraph 4 of the Introduction (see annex 1 below). Nonetheless it seems clear that the two documents have been drafted in a coordinate way and a market counterparty is therefore excluded.
[12] For a recent case involving an alleged conflict of interest in a conglomerate firm of solicitors, see *David Lee & Co. (Lincoln) Ltd* v *Coward Chance (a firm): Supasave Retail Ltd* v *Coward Chance (a firm)* [1990] 3 WLR 1278; [1991] 1 All ER 668.
[13] This is the method of conflict avoidance usually adopted in the public sector or elsewhere when an individual, as opposed to a firm, has a potential conflict of interest of this kind.

[14] See core rules 23 and 24.

[15] See Schedule 8, paragraph 3 as amended.

[16] There are two sets of regulations, one for most authorised persons, and one for chartered accountants. Some authorised persons (e.g. most LAUTRO members and solicitors) are not covered by either set.

[17] A nominee company is a mere 'holder' of the assets of another with no rights of management or decision making. A 'bare' trustee is the English phrase for a similar person whose duties come from a trust. Such a trustee is described in the Financial Services Act 1986, schedule 1, para. 22(1).

[18] 'Margin' is, broadly, a fidelity deposit in the derivatives markets; see further chapter 8, paragraph 25.

[19] It seems that the true construction of the principle is that the final phrase, 'in accordance with the responsibility it has accepted', qualifies 'proper protection'. The alternative construction, that it qualifies the choice between methods of proper protection, is a less natural one.

[20] See further core rule 13.

[21] Thus producing a similar result to the definition in the glossary.

CHAPTER 3

THE LEGAL SETTING FOR THE PRINCIPLES

Background

[1] One of the new powers given to the SIB in the Companies Act 1989 was the power to issue statements of principle 'with respect to the conduct and financial standing expected of persons authorised to carry on investment business'.[1] The purpose of this new power was essentially twofold. First, the intention was to bring into existence, in more or less permanent form, a compressed and quintessential summary of the general standards to be striven for. This was described[2] as 'the guiding light of firms engaged in investment business'. In view of the expected (and in the result achieved) high level of generality, it was provided in the Financial Services Act 1986, section 47A that the statements should be enforced more as a matter of discretion on the part of the regulators than as a matter of civil right vested in potential litigants. Accordingly, a breach of a statement of principle forms a ground for the exercise of disciplinary functions by the regulators, but does not of itself give rise to a right of civil action in the courts.[3] For the detail about enforcement powers in relation to principles, see paragraphs 20-26 below.

[2] The second purpose, allied to the first, was more structural. The 1989 reforms of the Financial Services Act 1986 created a new three

tier structure. This book describes the top and the middle tiers in the structure, i.e., the principles in Part A, and the so-called 'core rules' in Part B. The third tier is the support to be given by the self regulating organisations to the principles and the core rules. This comprises, as may be preferred by them, rules, guidance or codes of practice, and is required to produce to the satisfaction of the SIB an adequate level of investor protection. That third tier is outside the scope of this book.

[3] The 10 principles, as issued on 15 March 1990, and as brought into force on 30 April 1990, are set out in annex 1. Each of them is set out, one by one, in the detailed analysis in chapter 2.

APPLICATION OF THE PRINCIPLES

[4] The 10 principles have very wide application indeed. They apply to every firm which is authorised under the Financial Services Act 1986, whether by virtue of membership of a self-regulating organisation (SRO), or, as in the case of many solicitors, accountants, actuaries and investment brokers, by virtue of a certificate issued by the relevant professional body (RPB). They also apply direct to the 85 or so firms that are directly regulated by the SIB.

[5] There are, however, some inherent limitations on the scope of application, of which the following four are the most important. They relate to investment business (paragraphs 6 and 7 below), territorial scope (paragraphs 8-12), specific limitations (paragraphs 13 and 14) and time (paragraph 15).

[6] **Investment business.** In so far as the principles relate to business, as opposed to financial standing, they are limited in their application to 'investment business'. It would have made little sense, however, to have restricted the scope of principles as they affect financial standing, since experience in prudential supervision and in capital adequacy tends to show, as discussed in chapter 2, that matters affecting financial standing are indivisible. A threat to a firm's financial stability arising in one sector of its business is an equal threat to all other sectors.

[7] In relation to the conduct of business, however, the introduction to the principles declares that they apply directly to the conduct of investment business.[4] This distinction will not, of course, matter for

a firm such as a unit trust management company, since it is, by statute, not permitted to carry on any other business other than investment business.[5] On the other hand, for a bank or for a firm of solicitors, to take two examples, the distinction is of substantial importance. Ordinary banking business is not covered by the principles, since that aspect of a bank's affairs is neither investment business nor, indeed, regulated by the financial services regulators, but by the Bank of England under the Banking Act 1987. So, when it comes to deposit taking or overdraft facilities, an ordinary banking customer need not expect the bank to be responsive to, nor expect the bank's regulator to be concerned with the enforcement of, any of the specific provisions in the statements of principle. In so far as those statements of principle contain propositions that also have validity from other sources (e.g. from the common law of England and Wales or from Scots law), there may well be consonance, and conduct which is a breach of the principle may well be relevant to the application of the fit and proper test in the Financial Services Act 1986, but the principles themselves do not, strictly speaking, apply. Equally, when a solicitor is advising a litigant about his chances of success in the litigation, the principles do not apply; but, when he is advising that same client whether and how to invest the money obtained as a result of that litigation, that will ordinarily be investment business, and the principles apply.

[8] **Territorial scope.** The principles themselves, and, indeed the introduction to them, are silent on the question of territorial application. There is an implied limit, however, in that the principles apply to a firm if it is authorised under the Financial Services Act 1986. The requirement so to be authorised stems from the carrying on of investment business in the United Kingdom whether:

(a) by way of carrying on investment business from a permanent place of business maintained by the firm in the United Kingdom, or

(b) by way of engaging in the United Kingdom in relevant investment activities.

Case (a) above can be described as a 'UK based firm', and case (b) as a 'services firm'.

[9] In the case of the UK based firm, the principles clearly apply to the investment business carried on in the United Kingdom, and it

seems plain, on general principles, that this should remain so, even if the business is being done there for an overseas customer. It is not so plain whether the principles continue to apply when staff based in the United Kingdom physically go abroad and carry on investment business there. Nor, indeed, is it clear exactly what the position is when a UK based firm sets up a branch in a foreign country (or indeed when a foreign (UK authorised) firm does the same). There is as yet no reported authority on the application of the principle in any of those circumstances, and it is possible that this will continue to be an area lacking technical precision. The principles are themselves enforced at the discretion of the regulator (see below), and are expressly described as 'not exhaustive'.[6] Further, in relation to conduct which is as generally described as that in the principles, it is likely that any alleged breach overseas will be replicated by or related to other conduct which plainly has effect within the United Kingdom territorial jurisdiction.

[10] For instance, if an investment manager of a firm, based in the United Kingdom, had a policy that all discretionary portfolios managed by him would be charged on the same basis, but that discretionary portfolios managed for overseas customers would always be put into specific investments only after the best deals had been carried out for equivalent portfolios managed for United Kingdom clients, it seems likely that this would be regarded as a breach of principle 1 (integrity and fair dealing). Even if the wrong done arguably had effect only overseas, the conduct was organised and systematised within the United Kingdom.

[11] Similarly, with a services firm, it seems plain that the principles apply to any investment business carried on in the United Kingdom, that is the engaging in the United Kingdom in the relevant activities. It is not so plain whether ancillary business carried on in the overseas country by that firm is to be included. Common sense suggests that the principles should apply to such business done overseas only if it has some real and substantial connection with the United Kingdom, and it seems possible that, over time, some of the private international law about torts or delicts committed across international borders will be brought to bear. Imagine, for instance, that the services firm had the obverse of the policy described at paragraph 10. This policy, if lawful, would serve to put United Kingdom customers last, and would thus disadvantage them. That effect in the United

Kingdom would, it is suggested, be capable of challenge by the United Kingdom regulators, even if the decision to create that policy had been taken abroad. On the other hand, if the policy were to treat all portfolios alike, except only those where the customers lived in, say, Ruritania, and the Ruritanians were put behind the others, it seems likely that that policy could not, strictly, be challenged by a Ruritanian under principle 1.

[12] In one respect, the position has been expressly regulated by Parliament. An overseas operator of a UCITS scheme,[7] established, say, in Luxembourg or Dublin, was given a special authorisation under section 24 of the Financial Services Act 1986 for investment business involved in relation to that scheme. The 1986 Act makes it plain that the principles are to apply to such an operator only in relation to marketing in the United Kingdom.[8] If the analysis in paragraph 11 above is right, therefore, the result is that the overseas UCITS operator is less amenable to the jurisdiction involved in the principles than are other services firms. The definition of marketing in section 86(7) is fairly restricted, and matters covering the operation of the fund, for instance, do not in general fall within the scope of the principles.

[13] **Specific limitations on legislative power.** One such limitation (UCITS managers) has just been mentioned. There is a similar and rather more significant one relating to life insurance companies. The application of principles is specifically limited, in the case of a so-called 'regulated insurance company'[9] to the marketing of life policies and the management of the investments of pension funds.[10] Further, this restriction to marketing and pension fund management is applied, *mutatis mutandis*, to regulated friendly societies.[11]

[14] The consequence of this express restriction on scope deserves a little more analysis. First, principle 8 (financial resources) is plainly not relevant to regulated insurance companies and regulated friendly societies: the question of capital adequacy for firms of either of these categories is a matter for the Secretary of State for Trade and Industry or for the relevant Registrar of Friendly Societies.[12] The remaining nine principles apply in greater or lesser measure to firms in these two categories. For instance, principle 5 (information for customers) seems fully applicable to, and indeed to describe the quintessential nature of, marketing responsibilities, though the second sentence in

the principle, on accountability, has to be read in the light of the general limitation: that sentence in the principle could not be used so as to require an insurance company to report to the customer on the success or otherwise of its investment policy, at any rate outside the area of pension fund management. In similar vein, some of the other principles seem likely to be applicable only in rare circumstances. For instance, principle 7 (customer assets) is unlikely to have much application to a regulated insurance company except in respect of documents held, money in transit and, possibly, pension fund management.

[15] **Limitation in terms of time.** As mentioned above, the principles were made on 15 March 1990, and came into force on 30 April 1990. In accordance with normal principles of non-retrospection, this means that they should be regarded as having prospective effect only, i.e., in relation to acts or omissions on or after 30 April 1990.[13]

APPLICATION TO OTHER FIRMS AND PERSONS

[16] The power to make principles was expressed as being 'with respect to the conduct and financial standing expected of persons authorised to carry on investment business'. At first sight, therefore, it might be thought that other firms not actually authorised were not covered.

[17] **Appointed representatives.** In relation to appointed representatives, however, it seems clear that the principles have effect, since, by virtue of section 44(7) of the Financial Services Act 1986, the acts or omissions of an appointed representative are taken to be the acts or omissions of the authorised person. Accordingly, while the appointed representative cannot himself be disciplined by the SRO, the principal for whom he was acting can be.

[18] **Permitted persons.** The initial view is also too facile in the use of 'permitted persons', that is firms which have obtained from the SIB a permission to deal in investments without requiring authorisation. Most of the 150 or so permitted persons have applied for this particular status because of their treasury operations. The SIB expects them to abide by the principles or at least those which are relevant to the business covered by the permission, and would treat any lack of observance as capable of constituting grounds for withdrawal of the permission.

[19] **Application to individuals.** Even though each of them is actually directed at a firm, the principles can be enforced against an individual in a somewhat indirect way (see paragraph 23 below). It therefore follows that a failure by an individual to play his part in the compliance by a firm with a principle could be taken as relevant to an issue whether that individual is a fit and proper person to be employed in connection with investment business. In addition some of the SROs have taken steps to enable their disciplinary machinery to take into account breaches of the principles by registered individuals. Further, it can generally be expected that the compliance arrangements within the firm will ensure that the individuals are required, as an internal disciplinary matter, to have regard to and to comply with the principles.

ENFORCEMENT OF THE PRINCIPLES

[20] Failure to comply with a statement of principle under section 47A 'is a ground for the taking of disciplinary action or the exercise of powers of intervention, but it does not of itself give rise to any right of action by investors or other persons affected or affect the validity of any transaction'.[14] Accordingly, in general, the principles are enforceable:

(a) by the regulator only, and not by the investor;

(b) as a matter of regulatory discretion, and not as of right, and

(c) if it seems likely to be in the public interest, for the maintenance and improvement of standards, as a higher priority than redress.

[21] **Matter for disciplinary action.** Section 47A(4) sets out four types of discipline. As it turns out, however, the statutory discipline is available only relatively rarely, because so many of the firms concerned are in fact authorised by an SRO or by certification by an RPB. In most cases, therefore, the powers of the SRO or RPB will be more relevant (see paragraph 31 below).

[22] The disciplinary action set out in the statute is as follows:

(a) 'The withdrawal or suspension of authorisation under section 28 or the termination or suspension of authorisation under section 33'. These two powers, available to the SIB, are relevant only where:

(i) the person concerned is directly authorised by the SIB itself (section 25), or

(ii) the person concerned is a so-called 'Europerson', that is a person authorised, pursuant to section 31, to carry on investment business in the United Kingdom by virtue of being authorised in another member State of the European Community.

(b) 'The giving of a disqualification direction under section 59'. This is a wide power available to the SIB in respect of 'any individual'. The fact that the individual is, or works for a firm which is, authorised by an SRO or RPB does not remove the jurisdiction. The power is exercisable only if it appears to the SIB that the individual concerned is not a fit and proper person to be employed in connection with investment business, or investment business of a particular kind. The prohibition is that he is not, without the SIB's consent, to be employed in connection with investment business by any authorised person or any particular class thereof (e.g. any insurance company, or futures and options firm). Although, therefore, all 10 of the principles are specifically directed at 'firms', breach of them by a person in his capacity as the *alter ego* of a firm, or as a director, officer or employee of a firm, or, indeed, as (or employed by) an appointed representative, will necessarily be relevant to this form of disciplinary action.

(c) 'The making of a public statement under section 60'. This power, by contrast, is restricted to a narrow class of firms, that is those authorised by virtue of

(i) section 22 (insurance companies);

(ii) section 23 (friendly societies) if not a member of an SRO;[15]

(iii) section 24 (operator or trustee of UCITS scheme from another member State);

(iv) section 25 (persons directly authorised by the SIB); and

(v) section 31 ('Europersons').

Generally speaking, therefore, the power extends only to those who are regulated by the SIB in the conduct of their investment business.

But there is an exception to this implicit in the inclusion of insurance companies, whether they are members of the relevant SRO (LAUTRO) or not.[16]

(d) 'The application by [the SIB] for an injunction, interdict or other order under section 61(1)'.

That subsection gives power to the SIB[17] to take proceedings where there is a reasonable likelihood that any person will contravene any provision of the statement of principle. Equally the application may be made by the SIB on the ground that any person has contravened a provision of a principle and that there is a reasonable likelihood that the contravention will continue or be repeated. Thirdly, the application may be made on the ground that any person has contravened any principle and that there are steps that could be taken for remedying the contravention. The court has power under the subsection to make an injunction (or in Scotland an interdict) prohibiting the contravention. Alternatively, the court may make an order requiring the person found to have contravened and any other person who appears to the court to have been knowingly concerned in the contravention to take such steps as the court may direct to remedy it.

[23] Accordingly, the disciplinary action appears to divide into two distinct classes. Those at 22 (a) and (c) above are restricted, broadly speaking, to firms which are directly regulated by the SIB, though there is the additional point about insurance companies under (c). With much wider scope of application, however, are the powers at (b) and (d), each of which applies, not only to the area of investment business normally regulated by the SIB, but to the area normally regulated by the SROs and RPBs. The power at (b) relates to individuals, but the power at (d) relates to any person who is subject to any of the relevant provisions (in this case the principles) and also to any other person knowingly concerned in the contravention, whether specifically bound by the obligation in the principle or not.

[24] It is, therefore, possible that a firm or individual not carrying on any investment business could be made the subject of an order under section 61(1): this could happen if the court were satisfied that there had been a breach of the principle by an authorised firm, and that someone else had been 'knowingly

concerned' in the contravention. The financial backers of a dubious investment business, concerned to make money for themselves out of the arrangements set up by that dubious business, are an obvious example of this.

[25] So far as members of SROs or RPBs are concerned, therefore, the only disciplinary measures which could affect them in the ordinary way are those described at (b) and (d) above. There are, however, specific provisions made by SROs and RPBs applicable to them (see paragraph 31 below).

[26] **Challenge to disciplinary action.** It is convenient to take the last power (application for injunction or interdict) first. Plainly, since this action is a right to apply to the court, the correct place to challenge any use of the power is in the court itself. The remaining elements of disciplinary action are amenable to a reference to the Financial Services Tribunal. Any of the disciplinary action in (a) to (c) above is subject to the Tribunal's jurisdiction, to be invoked, at the election of any person affected, and in advance of the action taking effect. Accordingly, before authorisation is suspended, or withdrawn (or terminated), or a disqualification direction is given, or a public statement is made, the person affected has a right to refer the case to the Tribunal and the Tribunal is then required to investigate the case and to report to the SIB what would in its opinion be the appropriate decision in the matter, and the reasons for that opinion. It is then the duty of the SIB to decide the matter forthwith in accordance with the report of the Tribunal.

POWERS OF INTERVENTION

[27] Section 47A(3) refers not only to the taking of disciplinary action but to the 'exercise of powers of intervention'. Section 47A(4) then defines the powers of intervention as the powers conferred by Chapter VI of Part I of the Financial Services Act 1986. Again, from the point of view of a member of an SRO or RPB, it will be seen that the powers of intervention are themselves heavily restricted, and apply mainly, if not exclusively, to firms that are directly regulated by the SIB.

[28] The powers of intervention concerned can be unleashed on any one of three grounds, all of which seem relevant to a breach of principle. The three grounds for intervention are:

(a) that the exercise of the powers (in respect of a directly regulated person) is desirable for the protection of investors; or

(b) that the (directly regulated) person is not fit to carry on investment business; or

(c) that the (directly regulated) person has contravened a statement of principle.

[29] The various powers are set out in sections 65 to 68. Effectively, the SIB may take any of the following actions:

(a) it may restrict the nature of the person's business under section 65;

(b) it may restrict the directly regulated person from dealing with any of his assets, whether in the UK or elsewhere, under section 66;

(c) it may require the transfer of

(i) the assets of the directly regulated person, or

(ii) the assets of investors held to that person's order

to a trustee (section 67);

(d) it may require assets of an amount set by it to be maintained in the United Kingdom (section 68);

(e) it may (exceptionally) exercise the powers in (c)(ii) above in respect of another authorised person if the relevant SRO or RPB so requests.

[30] Again, the exercise of these powers is referable to the Tribunal, but with this difference that the action may be taken immediately, rather than only after the opportunity for the Tribunal to consider the matter further has been made available. Effectively, powers of intervention are exercisable by notice, whereas disciplinary action takes the form, initially, of a notice of intention to take action.

DISCIPLINE AND INTERVENTION BY SROs AND RPBs

[31] The various SROs and RPBs have taken action to enable their disciplinary and intervention systems to take account of breaches of principle. Generally, this has been done by making the principles a matter of direct obedience, and relevant to the 'fit and proper' test. In the case of some of the SROs, however, it is possible to foresee that a breach of a principle might also be relevant in the context of consumer redress, whether in the course of the disciplinary system itself or in other ways. It would, however, be beyond the scope of this book to give an exhaustive account of those arrangements: the reader is referred to the rule books of the relevant regulatory body.

[32] **Waiver**. Parliament envisaged, in section 47B of the Financial Services Act 1986, that the relevant regulatory body might be prepared, on the application of a member, to adapt a principle to the applicant's specific circumstances, or to dispense the applicant from compliance with the principle generally or for specific kinds of business. Since, however, the principles which emerged from the process are very general and 'high level', the Government has announced[18] that section 47B will not be brought into force as long as that degree of generality persists.

NOTES

[1] Section 47A of the Financial Services Act 1986, inserted by section 192 of the Companies Act 1989. The section refers to the Secretary of State, but the powers concerned have been delegated to the SIB by subordinate legislation.
[2] Official Report, House of Lords, 13 November 1989 at col. 1095 (Lord Trefgarne).
[3] Section 47A(3) of the Financial Services Act 1986.
[4] Paragraph 1 of the introduction reads:
These principles are intended to form a universal statement of the standards expected. They apply directly to the conduct of investment business and financial standing of all authorised persons ('firms'), including members of recognised self-regulating organisations and firms certified by recognised professional bodies.
[5] See section 83 of the Financial Services Act 1986.
[6] Introductory paragraph 2 of the principles reads as follows:
The principles are not exhaustive of the standards expected. Conformity with the principles does not absolve a failure to observe other

requirements, while the observance of other requirements does not necessarily amount to conformity with the principles.

[7] That is, a collective investment scheme (or Undertaking for Collective Investment in Transferable Securities) which is given a European 'passport' under the European Community Directive of 20 December 1985 (85/611/EEC).

[8] See section 86(7) (as amended by the Companies Act 1989).

[9] Basically this means insurance companies governed by Part II of the Insurance Companies Act 1982.

[10] See Schedule 10 to the Financial Services Act 1986, at paragraph 4 (as amended by the Companies Act 1989).

[11] See paragraph 14 of Schedule 11 to the Financial Services Act 1986 (as amended).

[12] That is the Chief Registrar of Friendly Societies (for Great Britain) and the Registrar of Friendly Societies for Northern Ireland (for Northern Ireland).

[13] The introduction to the principles, at paragraph 5, indicates that principles are really a restatement of existing standards: but also that the additional sanctions resulting relate only to matters occurring after 30 April 1990. Paragraph 5 of the introduction reads as follows: Although the principles may be taken as expressing existing standards, they come into force formally, with additional sanctions resulting, on 30 April 1990.

[14] Section 47A(3).

[15] The position about friendly societies is highly complex: the relevant provision in this case is paragraph 21 of Schedule 11 (as amended).

[16] The reason for this is that insurance companies to which section 22 applies (bodies authorised under section 3 or 4 of the Insurance Companies Act 1982 to carry on insurance business which is investment business, if carrying on such insurance business in the United Kingdom) obtain authorisation under the Financial Services Act 1986 only by virtue of that section and not, for instance, by virtue of membership of a recognised self-regulating organisation. This effect is achieved by paragraph 2(1) of Schedule 10 to the 1986 Act. Accordingly, life insurance companies have, in general, become members of LAUTRO, not because they require authorisation in that regard, but because they would prefer to participate in regulation as members of an SRO and in consequence to be governed in relation to their marketing etc. by the conduct of business rules of LAUTRO rather than by those of the SIB. As to this, see section 48(1) of the 1986 Act (as amended).

[17] Some of the powers conferred by the subsection have been retained exclusively or concurrently by the Secretary of State: see section 114(8) and the two relevant delegation orders.
[18] See Official Report, House of Commons, 26 October 1989 at col. 1239 (Mr Redwood) and Official Report, House of Lords, 13 November 1989 at col. 1095 (Lord Trefgarne).

PART B THE CORE CONDUCT OF BUSINESS RULES

CHAPTER 4

THE CORE RULES IN GENERAL

[1] Under the new arrangements established in 1989, 'core rules' are rules which are made by the SIB, but which have effect not only for persons directly regulated by the SIB, but also as rules binding on members of SROs.[1] In the new three tier structure, the core rules represent the second or middle tier. They state the essence of the obligations relating to conduct of business (and to three other areas described in Parts C and D below). They are designed to produce integrity of approach among all the relevant regulators, at an intermediate level of generality, that is below the level of the principles, but above the level of the specific elaboration of the core rules by the SRO itself. The statutory phrase used in conferring the power is 'designation', and in the subsequent stages 'core' and 'designated' are used interchangeably.

[2] Core rules do not apply to firms certified by RPBs. During the passage of the 1989 Act, it was frequently suggested that the RPBs should be brought within the scope of the power, but this did not commend itself to Parliament.

[3] At the present moment, the core conduct of business rules are not yet in force in relation to any SRO. The intention is that they should be brought into force, by a separate commencement order

made by the SIB, once the relevant third tier rules have been made in support of the core rules.[2]

[4] The core conduct of business rules, unlike the principles, give rise to civil liability in the same way as the conduct of business rules made by an SRO.[3] In general, this will mean that there is in the background the prospect of an action for damages under section 62 of the Financial Services Act 1986, except where that section has been disapplied under the new section 62A.[4]

[5] The 40 core conduct of business rules described in this Part were made by the SIB on 30 January 1991. The instrument is set out in annex 2, and the accompanying glossary is in annex 4. The 40 core rules are subdivided into seven sub-units, each of which is handled in the following seven chapters. The headings for the sub-units are, of course, included for editorial and stylistic purposes only, and have no legal significance of their own. Before taking the rules individually it may be helpful to describe briefly a major distinction in the rules relating to types of customer, and another relating to the business covered by the rules. 'Derogation' by SROs is also covered, and an account is given of the split in the operation of the rules as between private customers and the others.

Customers

[6] The core conduct of business rules divide the customers for whom investment business may be done into two major classes. These are the private customer and the non-private customer. As discussed further at paragraphs 13–15 below about half of the core rules apply to private customers only, with the others applying more generally.

[7] The private customer includes any individual who is not acting in the course of carrying on investment business: so all natural persons investing for themselves (or for their families or otherwise) but not by way of business, are covered. The only exception, for individuals, is where the individual is himself acting in the course of carrying on investment business. So, for example, a solicitor in sole practice with a certificate from the relevant Law Society, or a sole practitioner FIMBRA member, would be excluded as regards actions in the course of carrying on investment business.

[8] A private customer also includes so-called 'small business investors'. These are companies or partnerships or trustees who are not shut out by a definition of 'ordinary business investor'. If, by virtue of size (and the precise details about size appear in the glossary) a company or partnership etc. is an ordinary business investor, then it will be a non-private customer, if it is a customer at all. Core rule 39 also enables the precise border between private customer and non-private customer to be adjusted slightly by one or more of the SROs where the customer is sufficiently experienced to waive private customer protections and gives his informed consent.

[9] Not every person for whom investment business is done will be a customer. The glossary excludes a market counterparty as well as a beneficiary under a trust. Market counterparty is itself defined so that, for instance, one broker or broker-dealer dealing with another will be regarded as a market counterparty of the other unless one or other of them (or both) is dealing as agent for an identified principal.

Business

[10] The other major distinction in the core rules relates to business which is 'regulated business' and business which is not. In general (though this is dealt with in more detail in chapter 11) regulated business is investment business carried on from a UK base, wherever the customer is, and whether there is a customer or not. It also includes most (though not necessarily all) investment business carried on from a foreign base with or for customers in the United Kingdom. Business carried on from a foreign base for customers abroad is not 'regulated business', though it may still fall to be governed by some of the core rules.

Derogation, guidance and individual waiver

[11] Some of the core rules are described as having effect 'subject to any exceptions contained in the rules of an SRO . . .'.[5] The exceptions contemplated are those in the SRO's legislation which expressly disapply or qualify any particular core rule in relation to a specific description of member firms, customers, transactions or circumstances. So a rule made by an SRO will not be an 'exception' (as defined in the glossary) if it does not specify the individual core rule that is being disapplied or qualified, and if it does not use express (as

opposed to merely implied) words of disapplication or of qualification.

[12] Where the words enabling exceptions to be made do not appear (either in the core rule itself, or in core rule 40, or in a separate instrument), the core rule will apply to members of an SRO without any lessening of its legal effect, though the SRO can of course add greater precision and detail or additional requirements or both. The SROs also have power (in core rule 38(1)) to issue guidance to clarify the nature of the standards set by the core rules. Further, in respect of individual members who apply to it, each SRO has power, under the Financial Services Act 1986, section 63B, to adapt a core rule to the member's specific circumstances, or to dispense the applicant from compliance with the core rule generally or for specific kinds of business.

The dividing line between private customers and others

[13] On publishing the core conduct of business rules in January 1991, the SIB emphasised 'an important distinction between those' (that is the core rules) 'which apply whoever the customer is and those which are specifically designed to protect the private customer'.[6] This emphasis indicated that, in seeking to resolve the difficulties that had emerged over the original rule books (see chapter 1 above) the problem about institutional investors had been tackled. Of the 36 core rules which impose duties on firms,[7] 17 impose duties generally, and 13 only in relation to private customers. The remainder are split into paragraphs that apply generally or in relation to private customers. Of the 17, five are subject to the power of the SROs to make exceptions, and the same is true of two of the six split rules.

[14] A comparison between the SIB's conduct of business rules and the core rules indicates the extent to which protection previously more widely conferred has now been restricted, at core rule level, to private customers.[8] The tally is seven complete rules and two part rules. So the amount of the core rules that is concentrated on the private customer has been, broadly speaking, doubled.

[15] In the account in chapters 5 to 11, and in annex 2, this book follows the SIB's January 1991 booklet, and accordingly rules printed in italics apply only where a firm is providing investment services to a private customer.

NOTES

[1] See section 63A of the Financial Services Act 1986.

[2] This is the position in relation to core conduct of business rules: as Part C shows, core rules are already in force in relation to financial supervision.

[3] The same will also be true of the proposed new client money regulations so far as 'designated': see Part D below. Financial supervision core rules do not give rise to civil liability: see chapter 12 below. The remaining proposed set of core regulations (on cold calling) is really concerned to confer civil enforceability on conduct which would otherwise be unenforceable: see Part D below and section 56 of the Financial Services Act 1986.

[4] Section 62A provides, with some exceptions, that civil liability under section 62 is not available except at the suit of a private investor, and the definition of a private investor for this purpose is provided by the Secretary of State: see SI 1990 No. 489.

[5] This is the general phrasing, used in rules 13(4), 16(1)(b), 18(2), 19 (twice) 25, 32 and 39. There is, however, one rule with a different phrasing, that is rule 31 (reportable transactions) which starts 'unless otherwise provided by the rules of an SRO . . .'. The difference is that, in most cases where exceptions are permitted, the rule can be narrowed in its effect, but not wholly disapplied: but rule 31 can be disapplied by an SRO *in toto*.

[6] See the Introduction to the SIB's booklet 'Principles and Core Rules for the Conduct of Investment Business': January 1991.

[7] That is omitting core rules 36 (Chinese walls: safe harbour), 38 (Reliance on others: safe harbour), 39 (Classes of customer) and 40 (Application). Strictly, rule 29 (Stabilisation) cannot be omitted, since it imposes a duty; but its effect is that of a safe harbour and the total might therefore be 35.

[8] For those interested in the analysis, the precise position is as follows. (Rules that are newly restricted to private customers are in brackets: rules which are subject to potential SRO exceptions are asterisked).

Rules applying generally	Rules applying only to private customers	Rules not included (no duty)
1	[4]	36
2	5(4)	38
3	6	39*

Rules applying generally	Rules applying only to private customers	Rules not included (no duty)
5(1)(2)(3)	[7]	40
9(1)	[8]	
	9(2)	
13*	10	
15(1), (3)	11	
16(1)(b)* (2)	[12]	
19*	[14]	
20	[15(2)]	
21	16(1)(a)	
22(2), (3), (4), (5)	[17]	
23	[18(1)]	
24	18(2)*	
25*	22(1)	
26(1)(b)	26(1)(a),(2)	
28	27	
29 (see Note 7)	[30]	
31*	37	
32*		
33		
34		
35		

CHAPTER 5

INDEPENDENCE

General

[1] Under the heading of 'Independence' there appear four core rules, on inducements, material interest (often described as conflict of interest), soft commission (which, unless managed, can be a threat to independence in advising and acting for a customer in securities) and polarisation (one of the principal structural changes introduced under the Financial Services Act 1986).

[2] In the professional world, independence is highly prized, and the client must always come first. In the commercial world, there has been a long tradition of *caveat emptor* ('let the buyer beware') and relationships are usually those of counterparties. There is therefore no duty to do the best you can for the customer, as he is the person to whom goods and services are being sold or from whom they are being bought. Though this principle of wariness in relationships has been modified by the courts and by Parliament, the basic notion, in the world of pure commerce, is still that of the market. The law governing the transaction is generally the law of sale, not the law of trusts.

[3] This dichotomy between the professions and commerce is, of course, somewhat blurred when the law of agency is introduced.

Here, when A agrees to act for P, he assumes fiduciary duties in relation to P and those duties include a requirement to act in the best interests of the principal.

[4] Investment business has some of both substrata, that of the professions and that of commerce: it is also an area where, perhaps more than anywhere else, obligations of an agency nature are assumed. The Financial Services Act 1986 represents a further modification by Parliament and by use of powers conferred by Parliament. This, and subsequent instruments under it, have sought:

(a) to clarify the position where an agency relationship is assumed, and

(b) even where there is no agency relationship, to require standards somewhat higher than pure *caveat emptor*.

[5] The core rules thus have to fit into a complex underlying structure; they seek to produce (or carry forward) the modifications described above in a way that makes sense in the modern commercial world, particularly in the deregulated atmosphere following 'Big Bang' in 1986. The financial services industry is full of groups, of associates, of contractual arrangements and multiple capacity firms which, combined with the ebullient degree of innovation in the sector in recent years, makes for complexity: but this produces a countervailing need, to which the core rules aspire, of stating clearly and simply the underlying framework of obligations.

[6] It may be asked why the core rules should start with the concept of independence. One answer is that the requirements stemming from the four core rules are structural and apply to the whole way in which the investment firm concerned is organised to do business. A second, and perhaps better, answer, is that it appears to have been the intention of Parliament that a high premium should be placed upon the qualities of independence. The first four paragraphs in the Financial Services Act 1986 Schedule 8 (which lays down the principles applicable to the SIB's legislative provisions) relate to high standards of integrity and fair dealing, skill, care and diligence, subordination of the interests of the firm to those of its clients, and the due regard to be had to the circumstances of persons with whom the firm deals. Independence is therefore expressly referred to in one

of those four principles, and very near to the surface of the other three.

[7] The four core rules each emphasise a different facet of the concept of independence. Thus:

(a) you must not become dependent on gifts or inducements, or seek to seduce another from his duty to his clients (core rule 1);

(b) you must not allow a material interest of your own, or a relationship which gives rise to a conflict of interest, to deflect you from your duty to your client (core rule 2);

(c) you must not have arrangements which give you benefits by way of soft commission unless the customer is still just as well looked after, and knows about the benefits you are getting from putting his business in the way of others (core rule 3);

(d) in the packaged product business, persons who claim to be independent must be genuinely independent (core rule 4), and if they have a product of their own can sell it only if it is really better than anyone else's (this part of the polarisation concept is in core rule 17).

Inducements

Core rule 1

A firm must take reasonable steps to ensure that neither it nor any of its agents:

a. offers or gives, or

b. solicits or accepts,

either in the course of regulated business or otherwise any inducement which is likely significantly to conflict with any duties of the recipient (or the recipient's employer) owed to customers in connection with regulated business.

Types of customer – all
Types of business – all (regulated business or otherwise)
Type of duty – reasonable steps

[8] The underlying purpose of core rule 1 is to prohibit the giving or receiving of gifts and other inducements if these could be damaging to customers' interests. The firm must take reasonable steps to ensure that there is no transgression either by itself or by any agent, which means any person (including an employee) who acts on the firm's behalf. A gift or inducement is wrongful if it might reasonably be expected to cause the recipient to act in a manner likely significantly to conflict with any duties of the recipient (or the recipient's employer) to customers.

[9] 'Significantly' is designed to provide a *de minimis* threshold. Minor gifts or inducements, like normal Christmas presents, calendars or the like, would not involve any breach of the core rule: but of course the third tier rules or a firm's own internal instructions may be more demanding than this. The test of likelihood is an objective one: the outsider looking in has to form a view as to whether the recipient might be caused to act in the manner stated, and the duties against which the conflict is to be tested are duties 'to customers' rather than to any particular specific customer.

[10] Of relevance in this context is the special definition of 'inducement' in the glossary; this is relevant to two other provisions in the core rules, that is rules 3 and 18(2) (soft commission and disclosable commission). This combination of rules with the definition of disclosable commission produces a form of regulatory 'trade-off': disclosure is set against control over inducements. In effect the definition of inducement creates a 'safe harbour' from allegations of breach of the rule about inducements in respect of conduct dealt with by core rules 3 and 18(2). The safe harbour is available to the recipient and to the payer of disclosable commission, and to both parties under an existing or proposed soft commission agreement. It extends to disclosure carried out under SRO rules, which may be relevant bearing in mind that core rule 18(2) applies only to private investors, and therefore provides no safe harbour in relation to core rule 1 where the transaction is not with a private customer.

Material interest

> **Core rule 2**
>
> Where a firm has a material interest in a transaction to be entered into with or for a customer or a relationship which gives rise to a conflict of interest in relation to such a transaction, the firm must not knowingly either advise, or deal in the exercise of discretion, in relation to that transaction unless it takes reasonable steps to ensure fair treatment for the customer.

Types of customer – all
Types of business – advisory/discretionary (regulated business only)
Type of duty – not knowingly to transgress

[11] Core rule 2 builds on principle 6 (conflicts of interest), by providing the sanction of civil liability in a case where a firm is acting on an advisory basis or in the exercise of discretion in the knowledge that there is a conflicting interest. The conflicting interest may arise in one or both of two ways. The first is where the firm has an interest of its own in the transaction, and that interest is 'material' (an expression borrowed from the former rule book of the Securities Association, now the Securities and Futures Authority). The second is where the firm has a relationship which gives rise to a conflict of interest. The defence offered to the firm in the latter part of the rule tracks part of the equivalent provision in principle 6 though the principle goes on to give details of ways in which fair treatment can be achieved. It is perhaps unusual that the principle should be more detailed than the core rule: here is a case where, in a sense, the principle provides support for the second tier rather than the other way round.

[12] There may be a temptation to consider the limitation in this rule to advice and discretionary transactions (and, indeed to regulated business) as leaving the field clear elsewhere: but the core rule does not cut down principle 6, which continues to operate in its wide ranging way, and with its emphasis on not acting unfairly in relation to conflicts of interest or interests of the firm. Third tier support and, of course, common law rights and duties may also fill in the landscape further outside the area covered by the core rule.

[13] The definition of 'material interest' in the glossary, and paragraph 2 at the end of the glossary itself, provide two safe harbours on lines similar to those provided for core rule 1 above. The safe harbour is supplied in two halves, the first one on the same basis as in core rule 1 (material interest does not include disclosable commission or soft commission): the second way of building the safe harbour, in paragraph 2 of the glossary, operates in respect of the details in the rule dealing with relationships giving rise to a conflict of interest. In summary, therefore, the glossary definition of 'inducement' provides the safe harbour for 'material interest' (bilaterally with the customer) and paragraph 2 at the end of the glossary the safe harbour for 'conflict of interest' (involving a triangle).

Soft Commission

Core rule 3

A firm which deals for a customer on an advisory basis or in the exercise of discretion may not so deal through a broker pursuant to a soft commission agreement unless:

a. the only benefits to be provided under the agreement are goods or services which can reasonably be expected to assist in the provision of investment services to the firm's customers and which are in fact so used;

b. the broker has agreed to provide best execution to the customer;

c. the firm is satisfied on reasonable grounds that the terms of business and methods by which the relevant broking services will be supplied do not involve any potential for comparative price disadvantage to the customer;

d. in transactions in which the broker acts as principal, he is not remunerated by spread alone; and

e. adequate prior and periodic disclosure is made.

Types of customer – all

Types of business – advisory/discretionary (regulated business only)
Type of duty – absolute

[14] Soft commission (at least in present day volume) is a relatively recent phenomenon in the UK securities markets. It has grown substantially here since the end of fixed commission in those markets, and the growth has been based on United States practice. The commercial pressures leading to soft commission agreements are that the fund manager has a substantial amount of business to place, and is anxious to use that economic bargaining power to best advantage. The broker (or broker-dealer) is anxious to secure 'order flow', that is to have an assurance that he will get not less than a certain amount of business in a particular period from a particular client fund manager. These two drives generate an agreement, in the language of the glossary, whereby the fund manager receives goods or services (often information technology) in return for an assurance that not less than a certain amount of business will be put through or in the way of another person (that is the broker or broker-dealer).

[15] The securities industry was for long and still is seriously divided as to whether this new way of doing business is harmless, or could have malign influence, not only for individual customers, but also potentially for the market itself. Concern relating to customers centred on the question whether the services supplied were services that benefited the customers, whose business, after all, was that which was to generate the commission: there was also concern that customers did not know, and had not agreed, that the fund manager should operate in this way, receiving, as it were, extra benefits and services for himself as a result of the business done for his customers. The concern in relation to the market centred on the belief that a high percentage of 'soft' business in the market-place would make the market inflexible and unresponsive, because more and more business would be tied up and not exposed to competitive market forces. There was also, but separately, market concern over the practice (often described as 'soft for net') whereby market makers have an agreement with a fund manager guaranteeing them a certain volume of turnover from him in return for supplying goods and services, such as computer hardware etc.

[16] In the course of the consultation on this subject,[1] the SIB, with the assistance of other regulators and practitioners, concluded that

the provision of services to fund managers under soft commission agreements was just as legitimate as the provision of so-called 'traditional' research. Both were paid for out of customers' commission. The SIB therefore decided not to ban the practice of soft commission altogether, but to ensure that it was properly and responsibly handled, that is by ensuring that it helped in the provision of investment services to the customer, to whom adequate prior and periodic disclosure has been and is made. However it also decided that the practice of entering into a soft commission agreement with a market maker or other principal dealer for goods and services in return for order flow (colloquially known as 'soft for net') should be prohibited.

[17] This policy is carried through into core rule 3 accordingly. The prohibition is placed upon the 'fund manager' in the above analysis, and it is the fund manager who is described as 'the firm' in the core rule. No specific prohibition is placed on the 'broker', but the core rules nonetheless control the behaviour of brokers in two ways:

(a) they will not wish to enter into agreements in the knowledge that the other party to the agreement is prohibited by core rule 3 from dealing pursuant to the agreement; and

(b) in any event they will wish to conduct themselves so as not to leave themselves open to attack under core rule 1 or 2 (inducements and material interest) by straying beyond the 'safe harbour' which has been fashioned in connection with core rule 3 (soft commission).

[18] The five requirements in a.-e. in the rule are all cumulative, though condition d. will not apply in every case. Under condition a., the only benefits permitted under the soft commission agreement are goods or services which assist the fund manager's customers, this proposition being subject to a double test (of reasonably being expected to assist and in fact being used for that purpose). Goods and services would fall short of the first if they were fanciful or had a tenuous or unreal connection with the fund manager's business for his customers. An example would be a trip to a warm weather resort on the pretext that this was to enable the fund manager to assess an investment opportunity. Goods and services might satisfy the first test but not the second if they were not in fact deployed to the customer's benefit: an example would be computer equipment

(relating to investment prices etc. but used in the treasury part of the firm).

[19] In earlier draft versions of the core rule, it was proposed to state expressly that the goods and services should provide advice, research or analysis (or databases or software designed in support); that level of detail is now removed in favour of the more general wording in a. about '(assisting) in the provision of investment services'. Further detail can be supplied in the third tier if this is thought necessary. The SIB has stated that the rule does not permit a broker to provide a fund manager with cash rebates to pay for third party services.[2]

[20] Condition b. requires a soft commission house to agree to provide best execution to a customer, and thus goes beyond the requirements in core rule 22 (best execution). In brief, the soft commission broker has to assume a fiduciary obligation to act in the best interests of the fund manager's customers. Condition c. in effect requires the firm to be vigilant to ensure that the soft commission agreement does not do any actual or potential disservice to the customer. If, for instance, the customer is dealing in large size (i.e., his transaction is unusually substantial), he might well expect to get a specially favourable price from a market maker, better than those currently being quoted on the relevant market at the time. The fund manager must be satisfied on reasonable grounds that, if the business were put through the soft commission broker, there would be no potential for a customer to receive anything other than the very best possible terms. Alternatively, the 'methods' of dealing might pose a possible source of disservice to the customer. For instance, if the fund manager were obliged to disclose in advance whether the deal was on the soft basis or not, there would be a potential for comparative price disadvantage.[3] Condition d. deals with the problem, discussed at paragraph 15 above, of 'soft for net'. The condition prevents the soft commission agreement being applied to areas of business in which the broker is acting as principal and is remunerated by spread alone. This describes the remuneration arrangements for market makers, who live on the difference between their bid and their offer prices (i.e., 'the spread'). Some other firms which are not technically market makers do likewise. Effectively, therefore, market makers, in their capacity as such (and those other firms), cannot offer soft commission agreements to secure order flow. Where, however, in an integrated house, the agency arm puts a transaction through the market making arm,

there will be remuneration otherwise than by spread alone, and the condition in the rule will not apply. The other conditions in a.-c. and e. will, however, continue to apply to the integrated house, particularly c. (no potential for comparative price disadvantage).

[21] Under condition e., adequate prior and periodic disclosure must be made. The rule anticipates (though does not specifically require) that the disclosure to customers will be made by the fund manager. It can be expected that the third tier rules will go into rather more detail on this aspect.

Polarisation

Core rule 4

(1) A firm which advises a private customer on packaged products must either:

a. be a product company or its marketing group associate; or

b. do so as an independent intermediary.

(2) A firm which is a product company or its marketing group associate must not advise private customers to buy packaged products which are not those of the marketing group.

(3) A firm which acts as an independent intermediary in advising a private customer on packaged products must act as an independent intermediary whenever it advises private customers on packaged products in the course of regulated business.

(4) But where a firm acts as an investment manager for a customer, the core rule on polarisation does not prevent the firm from advising the customer on any packaged product.

Types of customer – private customers
Types of business – advice on packaged products (regulated business only)
Type of duty – absolute

[22] Core rule 4, with core rule 17, provides the bedrock of the much discussed 'polarisation' policy, which was and remains one of the principal features of the UK system of regulation in respect of 'packaged products'. Such products initially were life policies and units in regulated collective investment schemes (authorised unit trust schemes and recognised schemes): but the definition is now enlarged in these core rules to include investment trust savings schemes. Shares in investment trusts themselves are not packaged products for this purpose, but regarded more as securities. On the other hand the savings scheme (and shares acquired through investment trust savings schemes) will be a product in itself. On a 'look through' basis, a personal equity plan dedicated only to unit trust units and operated by the manager is treated as a packaged product: see core rule 17(6).

[23] The essence of the polarisation policy is that clarity as to the capacity in which a person deals is judged to be requisite in this part of the investment market, which, before 1988, was characterised by many advisory firms which claimed to be independent but in fact confined themselves to one product supplier or only a few product suppliers. The method of resolving that problem chosen by the regulators[4] was a structural split in the market-place. This divides those who are independent from those who are not, and avoids, or keeps to a minimum, the extent of any blurring between those two sectors. Thus core rule 4(1) states the classic division. A firm which advises a private customer on packaged products must be either on one side of the divide or on the other.

[24] Core rule 4(2), dealing with the product company and its marketing group associates, imposes a restriction that they may not advise private customers to buy packaged products from outside the group. If you produce packaged products and you advise a private customer to buy one, the advice must be restricted to your own products. Conversely, core rule 4(3) requires the firm which acts as an independent adviser to cast the net of advice much wider, and to act on an individual basis as an independent adviser on all packaged products on which it can advise. If you are an independent intermediary adviser for any private customer you must be an independent intermediary adviser for all your private customers. This rule does not oblige a firm to take on any particular person as a private customer; but if it takes him on for the purpose of advice on

packaged products it must do so on the independent basis. Core rule 4 does not explain further what the independent basis means: core rule 17 deals with this.

[25] The predecessor to paragraph (2) of core rule 4 was the subject of an adverse report from the Director General of Fair Trading in 1987 on the ground that it was seen as a restriction upon trade. Retail financial institutions, including some banks, with in-house packaged products, wished to be able to continue to offer the in-house product alongside other available products. In the event, however, the then Secretary of State decided that it did not and was not intended or likely to have to any significant extent an adverse effect upon competition.[5]

[26] Since April 1988, therefore, the policy of polarisation has been in general force for packaged products. It was always subject in some of the relevant rule books to an exception for portfolio management. That exception is restated[6] in core rule 4(4), which should be read in conjunction with the detailed provisions of core rule 17. Further, under the core rules, the polarisation policy is now restricted to private customers: under the earlier rules, it operated in theory across the board, though its main impact has been in relation to private customers at least outside the occupational pensions field.

[27] In late April 1991, just as this book went to press, the SIB announced[7] that it had embarked on a review of a number of issues in the area of retail regulation, including an appraisal of 'the continuing aptness of various elements of the regime of polarisation'.

[28] For a further discussion of polarisation, in the context of 'standards of advice', see core rule 17 below.

NOTES

[1] Consultative Paper No. 29 (October 1989), Policy Statement (July 1990), Consultative Paper No. 46 (November 1990).
[2] Soft Commission Arrangements in the Securities Markets: Second Policy Statement (February 1991), para. 9.
[3] See the Second Policy Statement at para. 6.
[4] It is often suggested in the press and elsewhere that the polarisation policy is a feature of the Financial Services Act 1986 itself: in fact,

though Parliament pointed in two places in that Act in the direction of polarisation, the policy was created by subordinate legislation under the Act, rather than in the Act itself. The two places where Parliament appears to have been adverting to such a policy are in section 44 (which contemplates at subsections (4) and (5) exclusive agency arrangements for appointed representatives) and paragraph 6 of Schedule 8 (which requires the SIB's conduct of business provisions to make proper provision for the disclosure by an authorised person of the capacity in which he enters into an investment transaction). A later statutory instrument amending Schedule 1 (but subject only to negative resolution procedure) is a further possible addition: see now note (6) to Schedule 1, para. 13.

[5] See the Financial Services Act 1986 (Delegation) Order 1987 (SI 1987/942), recital 7.

[6] The definition of investment manager goes somewhat beyond discretionary portfolio management, and covers the case where a person accepts responsibility on a continuing basis for advising on the composition of a portfolio. Thus work done for his advisory clients by, say, a stockbroker is not included in the polarised area as long as the stockbroker has accepted responsibility of oversight, and as long as he acts only on behalf of a customer. This last condition means that where the manager is acting also on his own account the expression investment manager is not apt: so the exception is not available to the manager who operates a fund consisting in part of his own money and in part of customers' money; nor to a 'manager' who owes duties to a product company as well as or instead of to a customer.

[7] 'Retail Regulation: issues for review' published by the SIB in April 1991.

CHAPTER 6

ADVERTISING AND MARKETING

General

[1] After dealing with major structural and independence matters in the first group of core rules, the instrument proceeds to advertising and marketing. This seems the next logical subject to tackle, from the point of view of the customer and of the firm, since advertising and marketing are the doors to new business.

[2] This group consists of nine core rules. Two are on advertising itself (Section A below); two on overseas business (Section B below) (marketing or introducing business outside the general territorial application of the rules); four on the content of and general obligations concerning communications (Section C below), and one relates to responsible use of the marketing channel formed by the existence of appointed representatives (Section D below).

SECTION A ADVERTISEMENTS

[3] The advertising rules themselves (core rules 5 and 6) are designed to state as simply as possible the central requirements for a complex and important topic. Some complexity is inevitable, because of the

structure of the underlying main legislation, including sections 57 and 58 of the Financial Services Act 1986 with their requirements for investment advertisements to be issued by or else approved by an authorised person. Account has also had to be taken of further requirements in the Misleading Advertising Directive[1] of the European Community which these core rules implement for the investment services industry.

Structure for advertisements in the core rules

[4] The 'lead concept' in core rules 5 and 6 is an 'investment advertisement' which is defined in section 57(2) of the Financial Services Act 1986.[2]

[5] The next concept, in descending order of generality, is the 'specific investment advertisement'. This is defined as 'an investment advertisement which identifies and promotes a particular investment or particular investment services': so it excludes anything that does not relate to a specific firm or product (e.g. generic advertising), and anything that does not both identify and promote anything specific. Thus a 'warm up' or 'image' advertisement is excluded, since it does not identify investments or services in particular; and a 'tombstone' (that is a statement that a particular deal has been done by particular firms) is excluded as long as it does not promote.

[6] The third class of investment advertisements is a subset of the specific investment advertisement, that is the 'direct offer advertisement'.[3]

[7] This concept replaces the former expression 'off-the-page advertisement' in the previous rule books. A direct offer advertisement includes a pre-printed or off-the-screen advertisement: so a direct offer advertisement can be in a tear-out form in a newspaper or magazine, in a leaflet picked up in a branch office or sent through the post, or the equivalent on a screen based medium.

[8] Each of these three layers of definition is therefore a subset of the one above, a 'direct offer advertisement' being both a specific investment advertisement and, of course, an investment advertisement.

Issue and approval of advertisements
(This rule has four paragraphs, treated separately.)

Core rule 5(1)

Where a firm issues or approves an investment advertisement, it must:

a. apply appropriate expertise; and

b. be able to show that it believes on reasonable grounds that the advertisement is fair and not misleading.

Types of customer – all
Types of business – all
Type of duty – absolute as to expertise: otherwise proof of reasonable belief

[9] **General duties on issue and approval.** Paragraph 1 relates to the issue and approval of investment advertisements, and imposes standards of expertise and quality on this function. Issuing and approval are separate functions, whose coexistence has caused some confusion in the past. The story begins with section 57(1) of the Financial Services Act 1986 which prohibits any person other than an authorised person from issuing (or causing to be issued)[4] an investment advertisement in the United Kingdom unless its contents have been approved by an authorised person. So an authorised person can issue an advertisement without approval. If any other person is to issue it (or cause it to be issued),[4] approval by an authorised person is required. Most of rules 5 and 6 impose parallel requirements on issuing and on approval, though there are two exceptions (in rule 5(3) and 5(4)(b)), the reasons for which are explained below.

[10] The purpose of paragraph 1 is to make it plain that appropriate expertise (whether direct or obtained by contract or consultancy) is required before performing either function: so a firm which knows little or nothing about futures (e.g. because it deals only in life

insurance) should be chary of approving an advertisement about futures: it risks breach of the rule if it does not apply expertise which is appropriate in relation to futures or selling futures.

[11] The firm must also 'be able to show' that it believes on reasonable grounds that the contents and presentation of the advertisement are fair and not misleading. This reversal of the burden of proof, with the burden being on the firm to 'be able to show', stems from the Misleading Advertising Directive of the European Community. For the advertisement to be fair and not misleading, it is not enough for each statement made in it to be factually accurate and fair in itself. The effect of the advertisement as a whole, and its presentation, must also pass the test.

Core rule 5(2)

Where a firm issues or approves a specific investment advertisement it must ensure that the advertisement identifies it as issuer or approver, and also identifies its regulator.

Types of customer – all
Types of business – all
Type of duty – absolute

[12] **Audit trail for advertisements.** Paragraph 2 applies to specific investment advertisements only, and requires the firm, when issuing or approving such an advertisement, to ensure that the advertisement identifies the firm as the issuer or approver, and also identifies the firm's regulator. This brings forward the substance of the present rule based requirements which lead to most investment advertisements containing the rubric 'issued/approved by XYZ Limited, a member of [SRO]'. The requirement is limited to specific investment advertisements, but, in any case of doubt as to whether the advertisement qualifies for that purpose, firms may think it best to play safe by including the rubric. There is no prohibition in the core rule on so doing for non-specific advertisements, though the effect of core rule 8 will need to be watched where the rubric is to be attached to an advertisement issued to a private customer outside the United Kingdom.

Core rule 5(3)

A firm must not approve a specific investment advertisement if it relates to units in an unregulated collective investment scheme.

Types of customer – all
Types of business – unregulated collective investment schemes
Type of duty – absolute

[13] **Advertisements for unregulated collective investment schemes.** Paragraph (3) prohibits approval of specific investment advertisements concerning units in unregulated collective investment schemes. An unregulated collective investment scheme is any collective investment scheme (as defined in the Financial Services Act 1986, section 75 and Schedule 1) which is not within the glossary definition (see annex 4) of 'regulated collective investment scheme'. Many of these are offshore, such as open ended investment companies or mutual funds not recognised in the United Kingdom under sections 86 to 88 of the Financial Services Act 1986. Others are onshore, but not in the form of authorised unit trusts. The justification for core rule 5(3) is to be found in the relatively tight controls imposed by the Financial Services Act 1986 on the marketing of unregulated schemes. The method of control then chosen by Parliament in section 76 over promotion of these schemes was to prohibit authorised persons from issuing or causing to be issued advertisements about them, and from advising or procuring persons to become participants in them. That prohibition extends to reissue of an advertisement as much as to the original issue. Certain gateways to allow promotion of these schemes are available under regulations made by the SIB under section 76(3), but these cannot extend to permit promotion to the general public.

[14] Section 76 is, however, silent on the question whether an authorised person could approve an advertisement of this kind. Approval is not the same as issuing or causing to be issued and does not necessarily connote advising or procuring persons to become participants. The gap is, therefore, filled as in the SIB's existing conduct of business rules by core rule 5(3).

[15] The prohibition in the paragraph is, exceptionally in core rules 5 and 6, limited to approval, and thus creates a different substantive

regime as between issue and approval. The prohibition on approval in core rule 5(3) is absolute: the prohibition on issue, however, in section 76(1) is itself subject to the gateways in the section 76(3) regulations, and also does not apply to single property schemes under section 76(4). The policy of the core rule is that any advertisement about schemes exempt under section 76(3) or about single property schemes under section 76(4) should be issued by an authorised person, since they cannot be approved by an authorised person. So the promoter of the scheme must himself be authorised (or must arrange for an authorised person to take full responsibility for the issue of the advertisement) if he wishes to advertise it within the limits permitted under section 76(3). In addition, this result is consistent with the exception in section 76(2) for advertisements *issued* by the authorised person to another authorised person or to a person mentioned in section 76(2)(b). In this way, the intention of Parliament, that the controls in section 76 should be effective, is preserved and the pattern laid down by the section applies to advertisements whether originally issued or reissued.

Core rule 5(4)

A firm must take reasonable steps to ensure that it does not issue or approve a direct offer advertisement for the sale of investments or the provision of investment services to a private customer unless the advertisement:

a. gives information about the investments or investment services, the terms of the offer, and the risks involved, which is adequate and fair having regard to the (UK or overseas) regulatory protections which apply and the market to which the advertisement is directed; and

b. offers derivatives or warrants only where the firm itself issues the advertisement and does so only to a customer for whom it believes on reasonable grounds the investment or investment services to be suitable.

Types of customer – private customers
Types of business – all
Type of duty – reasonable steps

[16] **Direct offer advertisements to private customers.** Paragraph (4) contains two separate sets of requirements. First, direct offer advertisements for the sale of an investment or the provision of investment services to private investors must give adequate and fair information about the investment (including the risks involved). Since a direct offer advertisement is one that contemplates that the investor may in substance accept the offer by returning the form, information about the terms of the offer is also required. It will be noted that the direct offer advertisement (as defined) may also invite the responding customer to make an offer to be accepted by the firm or another: this reflects the practice in the insurance industry and elsewhere. Even so, the advertisement must give information about the offer that is invited. The requirement to disclose the risks involved arises in all cases, not just where, say, the proposal relates to illiquid investments. All of this information is to be adequate and fair having regard to the regulatory protections which apply and the market to which the advertisement is directed. The rule operates on advertisements into the United Kingdom from overseas, and therefore has to contemplate the possibility that the relevant regulatory protections may in fact be those of another country.

[17] The second set of requirements in paragraph 4 relates to derivatives and warrants. It is additional to the requirements for adequate and fair information in paragraph a. In substance, the additional material amounts to:

(i) a prohibition on approving another's direct offer advertisement for derivatives or warrants, and

(ii) a requirement that a direct offer advertisement can be issued only to a customer for whom the firm believes the derivative (or warrant) or the services relating to derivatives (or warrants) to be suitable.

[18] There has been in the regulatory, rule books from the outset, a substantially higher degree of concern relating to the risks involved for private investors in trading in derivatives markets and in warrants. Such trading for private customers is comparatively small at present,[5] but the gearing implicit in most derivative contracts is recognised as a particular risk and as a feature that makes the markets unsuitable for many. Later in the core rules will be found

provisions about 'contingent liability transactions', that is derivatives transactions where the customer will or may be liable to make further payments, and this further highlights the degree of risk involved in these markets. These requirements make it likely that permitted direct offer advertisements for derivatives or warrants will take the form of leaflets or screen based messages issued to carefully selected customers rather than any form of general advertising.

[19] The specific reference to 'issue' in paragraph b. shows that it, like 5(3), draws a distinction between issue and approval: cf paragraph 15 above. For further provisions about risk warnings, see core rule 10 below.

Issue or approval of advertisements for an overseas person

Core rule 6

A firm must not issue or approve a specific investment advertisement which is calculated to lead directly or indirectly to an overseas person carrying on investment business:

a. which is not regulated business; and

b. with or for a private customer who is in the United Kingdom;

unless both the advertisement contains the prescribed disclosure and the firm has no reason to doubt that the overseas person will deal with investors in the United Kingdom in an honest and reliable way.

Types of customer – private customers
Types of business – all (but relating to overseas persons' services)
Type of duty – absolute

Advertisements for overseas persons: general

[20] Core rule 6 insists on two conditions before specific investment advertisements are issued or approved for overseas unauthorised persons. The two conditions are, broadly, disclosure of loss of United Kingdom protection, and 'no hint of problems'. In practice this rule

will normally apply in the area of approval, though it may govern issue in certain circumstances also, especially if a UK member of an international group is issuing advertisements on behalf of other members of the group. The overseas unauthorised person will need for his advertisement the approval of a UK authorised person. If he does not have that approval, he commits an offence; and, more immediately, his contracts will be unenforceable and liable to restitution proceedings under section 57(5). Issuing and approving firms will need to tread carefully in relation to this rule, since it applies to advertisements calculated (that is likely) to lead directly or indirectly to overseas (unauthorised) supply.

[21] The advertisement issued or approved in this way for the benefit of any overseas unauthorised person must contain the 'prescribed disclosure' that is, broadly, a statement to inform United Kingdom investors of the loss of UK protection including, where relevant, loss of rights to UK compensation on default. The actual content of the prescribed disclosure is set out more fully in the glossary. Secondly, the advertisement must not be issued or approved if the firm which issues or approves has any reason to doubt that the overseas person will deal with investors in the United Kingdom in an honest and reliable way. So the 'overseas bucket shop' should find that the authorised community in the United Kingdom is unwilling to take on the responsibility of vouching for the advertisement (which will include, of course, compliance with core rule 5) once there has been any adverse publicity about dishonest or unreliable dealing. The consequence for a firm going ahead with approving an advertisement once it has any reason to doubt honesty or reliability of the overseas operation could be severe, since it would not be difficult to show under section 62 of the Financial Services Act 1986 that investors who lose money as a result of the promotion of the identified product or service in the advertisement have suffered 'loss as a result of the contravention of' core rule 6. The giving of prescribed disclosure will not avail the firm in such a case, since the core rule requires more of it than that.

[22] The rule is limited to specific investment advertisements, and therefore also includes the direct offer advertisement. Investment advertisements that are not specific, that is because they do not both identify and promote a particular investment or particular investment services, are not covered by the rule: but such advertisements

are still subject to the requirement for issue or approval in section 57 of the Act, and core rule 5(1) (fair and not misleading) will still apply to it. Core rule 40 contains specific provision about reissue of advertisements originally issued by another.

SECTION B OVERSEAS BUSINESS

Overseas business for United Kingdom private customers
(This rule has two paragraphs, treated separately.)

Core rule 7(1)

A firm must not carry on investment business:

a. which is not regulated business; and

b. with or for a private customer who is in the United Kingdom;

unless it has made the prescribed disclosure to the customer.

Types of customer – private customers
Types of business – all
Type of duty – absolute

[23] **Overseas business for United Kingdom private customers: disclosure.** If a firm is authorised, but does business for a United Kingdom private customer in such a way as to fall outside the territorial scope implicit in the meaning of 'regulated business', the customer must be given the 'prescribed disclosure'. On this see paragraph 21 above; broadly he must be told that all or most of the United Kingdom regulatory protections will not apply.

[24] The territorial application is derived from the definition of 'regulated business' in the glossary. So far as customers in the United Kingdom are concerned (and core rule 7(1) applies only for such customers who are also private customers) almost all business done by a firm is likely to be regulated business. The core rules apply to business carried on for such customers from an office of the firm abroad unless that office could escape the need for UK authorisation

in respect of that business if it were a separate person. A relevant exception, however, would be where the overseas branch of the authorised firm was able, pursuant to the inward marketing 'windows' in paragraphs 26 and 27 of Schedule 1 to the Act, to obtain the business of the UK private investor without requiring UK authorisation. Broadly, the UK investor must have started the ball rolling himself, or else responded to a lawful advertisement or 'cold call': the reader is referred to the fuller textbooks if he needs more than this amount of detail.

Core rule 7(2)

A firm must not give an introduction or advice, or make arrangements, with a view to another person carrying on such business with or for such a customer, unless it has both made the prescribed disclosure and has no reason to doubt that the customer will be dealt with in an honest and reliable way.

Types of customer – private customers
Types of business – all
Type of duty – absolute

[25] **Overseas business for United Kingdom private customers: introduction overseas.** Core rule 7(2) is, in a sense, a combination of core rules 6 and 7(1). It applies the 'disclosure' and 'no hint of problems' requirement in rule 6 to things done by an authorised firm with a view to unregulated business being done abroad for a United Kingdom private customer. Those things done by the authorised firm which are prohibited acts (unless core rule 7(2) is complied with) are introductions, the giving of advice and the making of arrangements with a view to another person carrying on that business. Broadly, therefore, the policy intent of the paragraph is that UK private customers' business should not be channelled abroad in a way which leaves them in the dark as to the potential consequences for good or ill.

[26] The primary impact of this prohibition will relate to introductions etc. to overseas unauthorised persons, typically a foreign subsidiary (or parent or fellow-subsidiary). It may also apply where the introduction, advice or arrangements are with a view to another

authorised person in the United Kingdom or, indeed, authorised person overseas, carrying on the unregulated business for the private customer.

Business conducted from an overseas place of business with overseas customers

Core rule 8

If, in any communication made or advertisement issued to a private customer outside the United Kingdom in connection with investment business which is not regulated business, a firm indicates that it is an authorised person, it must also, and with equal prominence, make the prescribed disclosure.

Types of customer – private customers
Types of business – all (unregulated business)
Type of duty – absolute

[27] Core rule 8 forms the fourth element in a quartet consisting of 6, 7(1), 7(2) and 8. Of those, two relate to UK authorised firms doing things in the UK to assist overseas business (6 and 7(2)); and two relate to UK authorised firms doing things overseas themselves (7(1) and 8). Rule 8, like rule 7(1), is a rule requiring disclosure only, rather than that plus the 'no hint of problems' condition to be found in the other pair in the quartet.

[28] The rule operates only where a firm chooses to indicate to a private customer that it is an authorised person: it is then required to state the prescribed disclosure. Since the rule is triggered by a statement, it requires the counter-statement to be made 'with equal prominence'. As with rule 7(1), the broad territorial scope of 'regulated business' means that the provision will only relatively rarely be operative.

SECTION C COMMUNICATIONS

Fair and clear communications
(This rule has two paragraphs, treated separately.)

Core rule 9(1)

A firm may make a communication with another person which is designed to promote the provision of investment services only if it can show that it believes on reasonable grounds that the communication is fair and not misleading.

Types of customer – all
Types of business – all
Type of duty – proof of reasonable belief

[29] **Fair and not misleading.** Rule 9(1) provides an echo of rule 5(1) b., applicable, however, not simply to investment advertisements, but to communications with other persons designed to promote the provision of investment services. As before, this provision is designed to implement, for this sector, a requirement of the Misleading Advertising Directive of the European Community, whose scope goes somewhat wider even than the concept of an advertisement in the Financial Services Act 1986.

[30] 'Communication' is undefined, but presumably will be taken to include oral as well as written or screen based communication. This conclusion is inescapable having regard to the inclusion of 'written' in core rule 9(2). The sole tests therefore will be whether the words or image or figure etc. amounted to a communication, and, if so, whether the communication was 'designed to promote the provision of investment services'.

Core rule 9(2)

A firm must take reasonable steps to ensure that any agreement, written communication, notification or information which it gives or sends to a private customer to whom it provides investment services is presented fairly and clearly.

Types of customer – private customers
Types of business – all
Type of duty – reasonable steps

[31] **Presented fairly and clearly.** By comparison with core rule 9(1), and subject to a point about writing (see below), core rule 9(2) goes wider in relation to the documents etc. covered, but less wide in terms of the persons protected. All agreements, (written) communications, notifications and information given or sent are covered, whether or not they are designed to promote the provision of investment services. On the other hand, it is only if they are given or sent to a private customer (to whom the firm provides investment services) that the duty to be fair and clear arises. The restriction to 'written' material is express only in relation to communications. But it is hard to see the rule being relied upon in civil proceedings in relation to an oral agreement, which can scarcely be 'presented'. The same is true of information, while notification appears to assume that there will be a written document of some sort. It is submitted, therefore, that the qualification of communication with 'written' does not affect the general drift of the rule which relates primarily to documents and other written material, including screen based messages.

Customers' understanding

Core rule 10

A firm must not recommend a transaction to a private customer, or act as a discretionary manager for him, unless it has taken reasonable steps to enable him to understand the nature of the risks involved.

Types of customer – private customers
Types of business – advisory and discretionary
Type of duty – reasonable steps

[32] **Understanding of risk.** This rule imposes a positive duty to take reasonable steps to enable the customer to understand the nature of the risks involved (core rule 5(4) spoke of 'the risks involved' and therefore, by inference, covers size as well as nature). It combines two rather different circumstances, that is a recommendation and discretionary management. On the former, it appears to be contemplated that the recommendation will be made only at the end of a period of discussion (or exchange of communications) between the firm and the private customer, in the course of which the reasonable steps will be taken to enable the customer to understand the nature

of the risks involved. So 'recommend' means, here, 'reach the end of a process of recommendation'.

[33] With the discretionary manager, the position will be somewhat different, as one of the features of a discretionary arrangement is that the customer will almost certainly not be asked to approve or even be informed about the transaction in advance. So the rule contemplates that the reasonable steps will have been taken at an earlier stage, typically in the discussions leading to and in the form of the 'two-way' customer agreement required for discretionary management of a private customer's investments by core rule 14(2), or any variation in that agreement which may be required if additional or different risks are to be taken on. Discretionary manager is undefined, but appears apt to include the case where the portfolio manager sells to or buys from the portfolio as principal as well as the more usual arrangements.

[34] In both cases (advisory and discretionary) the obligation is to take reasonable steps to enable the customer to understand the risks involved. This is an objective test in one sense, but focusing on the specific circumstances of the individual customer. So different explanation may be needed for a new or apparently slow-witted customer compared with that for a seasoned or alert one. The firm does not have to ensure that the customer understands the risks, merely that he has been enabled to understand. Where, however, the explanation is given in a misleading or disingenuous fashion, it is likely to be taken as insufficient to enable him to understand the risks. The third tier may well enlarge upon the most practical ways to comply with the generality of the core rule.

Information about the firm

(This rule has two paragraphs, treated separately.)

Core rule 11(1)

A firm must take reasonable steps to ensure that a private customer to whom it provides investment services is given adequate information about its identity and business address, the identity and status with the firm of employees and other relevant agents with whom the customer has contact and the identity of the firm's regulator.

Types of customer – private customers
Types of business – all
Type of duty – reasonable steps

[35] **Information about the firm: general.** This paragraph provides a list of information required adequately to be given to private customers. The implication is that the information should have been given before or during the provision of investment services. The list is adequate information about:

(a) the identity of the firm;
(b) the business address of the firm;
(c) the identity (and status with the firm) of employees with whom the customer has contact;
(d) the identity (and status with the firm) of other relevant agents (e.g. an appointed representative) with whom the customer has contact;
(e) the identity of the firm's regulator.

Relevant, in relation to an agent, is used to show that agents are included only where the contact with the investor relates to the investment business concerned. The information can be supplied in any way that seems reasonable: the more specific rules which this provision replaces dealt separately with notepaper, business cards etc. but, at the level of a core rule, the more general substance is now provided.

[36] Where more than one firm provides separate investment services to a single private customer, the obligation will lie upon each of them, though each will be able to rely on the other pursuant to rule 38(3) (communications supplied or to be supplied by another person). In practice, as long as the information is supplied by one or the other, the courts are likely to conclude that reasonable steps have been taken, and, in any event, the rule is relatively easy to comply with by sensible decisions on production of stationery and staff training.

Core rule 11(2)

Unless a firm is acting as an investment manager, it must take reasonable steps to ensure that a private customer it advises to buy a packaged product is also given adequate information about the firm's polarisation status, the buying process and any limits on the packaged products on which it can advise.

Types of customer – private customers
Types of business – advice to buy packaged products
Type of duty – reasonable steps

[37] **Information about the firm: packaged products.** This paragraph applies only where a firm is advising a private customer to buy a packaged product. 'Buy' has the extended definition in paragraph 28(1)(d) of Schedule 1 to the Financial Services Act 1986, and, where the transaction is one of exchange, it can be regarded as a transaction of purchase as well as of sale, and therefore within the rule.

[38] The firm must give adequate information about its polarisation status (that is whether it is a product company or marketing group associate under rule 4(1) a. or an independent adviser under rule 4(1) b.). Information also extends to the buying process, which appears to exclude anything about the packaged product itself, that being covered by core rule 12. This phrase is taken as a reference to the 'Buyer's Guide', as introduced into the relevant rule books in 1989-90, which deals with matters such as the duties of the adviser, cancellation rights, details of the product and surrender values. SRO rules and guidance are expected to provide supplementary material to assist their members to comply with this rule.

[39] The third area for the supply of information is 'any limits on the packaged products on which it can advise'. These may be limits based upon the polarisation rule (rule 4), or a reference to the limits envisaged by Parliament in section 44(4) and (5) (contracts between appointed representatives and principal): it may also apply to restrictions of a regulatory kind, stemming from membership of an SRO or categorisation within a class of membership. It appears also to contemplate responsible, self-imposed limits based on an acknow-

ledgment of a lack of full capability on the part of the adviser. Under core rule 17(1) (b), the independent adviser must take reasonable steps to inform itself about what packaged products are generally available on the market and on which it can advise. On the other hand, the firm with the opposite polarisation must take reasonable steps to inform itself fully about packaged products available from the marketing group and rule 17(4) contains the concept of products of which such a firm reasonably should be aware. Core rule 11(2) thus contemplates that, in principle, advice available should be as wide as in the context of core rule 17 including its concept of reasonable steps. On the other hand, the limits to be disclosed under 11(2) are limits on packaged products only: there is no need to mention any limits in respect of other products. In substance, therefore, core rules 11(2) and 17 admit of the possibility that independent financial advisers, and perhaps, to a more limited extent, tied advisers, may be specialised into sectors or otherwise; but if they are, they must disclose the speciality.

Information about packaged products
(This rule has two paragraphs, treated separately.)

Core rule 12(1)

Before or when making a personal recommendation to a private customer to buy a packaged product, a firm must give him information about the product which is adequate to enable him to make an informed investment decision.

Types of customer – private customers
Types of business – advice to buy packaged products
Type of duty – absolute

[40] Information at point of recommendation. This paragraph relates to product information. This is a subject of considerable complexity and detail in the third tier (principally LAUTRO) and, indeed, in the SIB's own product regulations concerning authorised unit trusts. The paragraph tracks fairly closely the language of paragraph 7 of Schedule 8 to the Financial Services Act 1986[6] and, indeed, principle 5 (information for customers).

[41] Information required is information about the product, but it has to be adequate to enable the customer to make an informed investment decision. The paragraph, being subjective to that extent, assumes, as seems reasonable bearing in mind core rule 16 (suitability), that a 'know your customer' process will have been gone through. As earlier discussed, in the context of principle 4 (information about customers), there is a principle based obligation which requires the adviser to seek from a customer information about him which might reasonably be expected to be relevant in enabling the adviser to fulfil his responsibilities to the customer. That principle, this paragraph and core rule 16 therefore appear to mesh closely together. Equally, it seems clear that simply passing on the product particulars supplied by the product company may not invariably be sufficient, if that does not give enough information to enable that customer to make an informed investment decision in his circumstances.

Core rule 12(2)

Before or as soon as practicable after a private customer buys a packaged product in a transaction recommended, effected or arranged by a firm, the firm must provide him with appropriate written product particulars unless:

a. the firm buys the packaged product as a discretionary investment manager; or

b. the transaction is effected or arranged on an execution-only basis.

Types of customer – private customers
Types of business – advising/arranging/effecting transactions to buy packaged products
Type of duty – absolute

[42] **Information at point of sale.** This paragraph of core rule 12 deals with written product particulars at the point of sale. The particulars concerned will generally be the (life company generated) product particulars compiled in accordance with the detailed LAUTRO rules, or the 'scheme particulars' for authorised unit trusts etc. compiled in accordance with the SIB's own product regulations.

[43] In relation to recommendations, paragraph (2) is something of a safety net: if the product particulars have been supplied under paragraph (1), the adviser plainly need not supply them again in the ordinary way at the point of sale. The rule will have been complied with on the 'before' basis. It would be seen as 'appropriate' to supply further product particulars at the point of sale after they had earlier been supplied at the point of recommendation only if the particulars had been changed in the interim. Equally, the recommender is under no obligation to provide the particulars himself if he believes on reasonable grounds that they will come to the purchaser direct from the product company (in this connection core rule 38(3) is relevant in avoiding duplication). This is so whether that company is actually authorised in the UK or not.

[44] For transactions effected or arranged by the firm, paragraph (2) exists on its own, without any prior requirement in paragraph (1). There is, however, an exception for the firm which deals in the exercise of discretion. If the customer is relying upon the discretionary portfolio manager for the selection, he need not be given product particulars on every occasion, as his rights to information will come from other core rules. A further exception relieves the firm if the private customer asks for the product on an execution only basis, that is without any advice or 'suitability' testing by the firm: if the customer has chosen his own product and buys it as if it were an orange or newspaper chosen by him, the firm need not give him additional paper to describe the nature of the product.

SECTION D APPOINTED REPRESENTATIVES

Appointed representatives

Core rule 13

(1) A firm must satisfy itself on reasonable grounds and on a continuing basis that any appointed representative it appoints is fit and proper to act for it in that capacity.

(2) A firm must also satisfy itself on reasonable grounds and on a continuing basis that it has adequate resources to monitor and enforce compliance by its appointed representatives with high standards of business conduct.

(3) A firm must ensure that any of its appointed representatives carries on regulated business for which the firm has accepted responsibility only:

a. in circumstances where the representative does not carry on (or purport to carry on) in the United Kingdom any investment business for which the representative is not an authorised or exempted person; and

b. in a way which ensures that the business for which the firm has accepted responsibility is, and is held out as being, clearly distinct from any financial business which the representative carries on which is not investment business, unless that other financial business is covered by authorisation under an enactment as a bank or building society;

but a firm does not break this requirement if it can show it has taken reasonable steps to comply with it.

(4) Subject to any exceptions contained in the rules of an SRO of which it is a member, a firm must ensure that its employment of any of its appointed representatives can be terminated only with the authority of its regulator.

Types of customer – all
Types of business – any business which appoints appointed representatives
Type of duty – reasonable grounds (paragraphs (1) and (2)): absolute (the rest but subject to a reasonable steps defence in (3))

[45] **General.** This core rule establishes, on a formal footing, a 'mini-regulatory regime' for appointed representatives. Section 44 of the Financial Services Act 1986 established a basis for a firm-based (rather than regulator-based) structure for control over and responsibility for retail and delivery mechanisms. This was intended mainly, though not exclusively, for the retail delivery of packaged products, and the expectation may well have been that the arrangements would be used to take on small corporate or individual enterprises in the intermediary sector. The subsequent use of the section to take on some of the High Street 'giants', as opposed to smaller advisory firms,

may have been surprising to some if not all of the authors of the section.

[46] The structure envisaged by the Act was one of agency, which was either an exclusive agency arrangement or one which could be converted by the principal into an exclusive agency arrangement. The principal would accept responsibility for the investment business of the agent. That acceptance of responsibility would be written (though not necessarily in the contract of appointment of the agent). The principal would also, as a matter of law, be responsible 'to the same extent as if he had expressly authorised it, for anything said or done or omitted by the representative'. Under the section, acts or omissions of the agent within the scope of the agency arrangement would be treated as the acts or omissions of the principal.

[47] The section contained no formal requirement for vetting by the principal of the fitness and propriety of the agent. But, since the acts and omissions of the agent were to be imputed to the principal, common sense and commercial best practice would suggest that there should be a fair amount of careful vetting, and the setting up of a structure on the part of the principal to ensure that the imputed liability in respect of the agent did not prove disastrous for the principal. In the early years of operation of the Act, it has become apparent that additional effort might well be required here, and that commercial pressures to have a sales network may have spoken more loudly to some product companies than the commercial risks of taking on unsatisfactory agents. LAUTRO, and the firms regulated by them, have in recent times devoted more attention to this subject, and the core rule is intended to state the emerging best practice.

[48] As mentioned above this core rule amounts virtually to a 'mini-regulatory regime', with arrangements for admission, monitoring, scope of operation, clarity of the border of the scope of operation, and arrangements for termination of the contract. Thus paragraph (1) has a 'fit and proper' test at the outset and on a continuing basis. Paragraph (2) contains a requirement for resources to monitor and enforce compliance by the agent. This, again, is at the outset and on a continuing basis. It echoes, though somewhat faintly, the equivalent monitoring and enforcement obligations of self-regulating organisations.[7]

[49] Paragraph (3) in effect requires the principal to ensure that his agent operates within the agreed 'scope' in circumstances where he does not carry on any unauthorised or unexempted investment business: and so as to ensure that there is a clear dividing line between the business done within that 'scope' and (subject to exceptions discussed at paragraph 50 below) any other financial business. The principal must police the border, and the border must be clearly defined. Further, the principal can not just restrict his attention to the business done within the agreed and accepted 'scope'; he must make sure that the agent is not operating (or giving signals about operating) in a way that is in fact unlawful. In the first years of operation of the appointed representative system, there has been a certain amount of difficulty about appointed representatives carrying on investment business in respect of which they appeared to be (but were not) within the scope of an agency arrangement. Difficult questions have then arisen about ostensible authority, and about where a loss should lie (on the insolvency or disappearance of the representatives) as between two more or less innocent persons (that is the investor and the principal). Secondly, difficulty has arisen in relation to appointed representatives, carrying on allied financial business for which no investment business authorisation is required, in circumstances that have led their customers to believe that they were acting as an agent for the relevant (authorised) principal and in a manner that was regulated by the law on investment business. Deposit taking, debentures sold in relation to property deals and capital release from property have been examples.

[50] The core rule requires a clear distinction to be drawn between this other financial business and business within the scope of the agency arrangement. Financial business is defined as business which is, or is held out as being, primarily for the purposes of investment. But that 'membrane' is not required in a case where the other financial business is covered by authorisation as a bank or building society. The rule does not require the clear distinction to be drawn in such cases, since both aspects of such a business are (and are understood to be) regulated in one way or another.

[51] Under paragraph (4), the employment of the appointed representative is to be terminated only with the authority of the regulator except where SRO rules make exceptions. This implies in the ordinary way, therefore, the involvement of the regulator in any case of termination. The underlying purpose relates to discipline and

redress: if the contract between the principal and the agent has been discharged, there would then be no more scope for quasi-regulatory oversight on matters where continuing access to records and accountability may be important. The paragraph speaks of the whole contract of employment of the appointed representative, rather than mere interruption of the contractual arrangement for delivery or supply of services. In many cases there will be no difference, but the core rule is concerned mainly about responsibility rather than about commercial supply. There is presently pending litigation on the question whether, and under what conditions, a regulator can affect the supply, pursuant to a contract, of agency services for one of its members.[8]

NOTES

[1] Council Directive of 10 September 1984 relating to the approximation of the laws, regulations and administrative provisions of the Member States concerning misleading advertising (84/450/EEC).

[2] Section 57(2) reads: 'In this Act "an investment advertisement" means any advertisement inviting persons to enter or offer to enter into an investment agreement or to exercise any rights conferred by an investment to acquire, dispose of, underwrite or convert an investment or containing information calculated to lead directly or indirectly to persons doing so.' This takes the reader to section 44(9) which reads as follows: 'In this Act "investment agreement" means any agreement the making or performance of which by either party constitutes an activity which falls within any paragraph of Part II of Schedule 1 to this Act or would do so apart from Parts III and IV of that Schedule".' As to 'advertisement', section 207(2) provides a wide but essentially self-centred definition ('includes every form of advertising, whether . . . or in any other manner'). The expression 'investment advertisement' is therefore pretty wide, and somewhat more extensive than the alternative formulation in section 48(2)(e) of 'advertisements in respect of investment business'.

[3] The glossary defines a direct offer advertisement as a specific investment advertisement (including a pre-printed or off-the-screen advertisement) which:

(a) contains:

(i) an offer by the firm or another offeror to enter into an investment agreement with anyone who responds to the advertisement; or

(ii) an invitation to anyone to respond to the advertisement by making an offer to the firm or another offeree to enter into an investment agreement; and

(b) specifies the manner or indicates a form in which any response is to be made (for example by providing a tear-off slip).

[4] In the core rules, 'issue' includes 'cause to be issued': see glossary.
[5] The estimates made periodically for the purposes of the Investors Compensation Scheme show what a relatively small proportion of business done in derivatives markets is done for private customers, which in this context means those who would be eligible to claim on the scheme if the authorised firm were to default.
[6] Paragraph 7 of Schedule 8 requires the SIB's relevant rules 'to make proper provision for requiring an authorised person who . . . gives any person advice about . . . a transaction, to give that person such information as to the nature of the investment and the financial implications of the transaction as will enable him to make an informed decision.'
[7] Financial Services Act 1986, Schedule 2 paragraph 4. An SRO is required to monitor compliance with its rules and with any legislative provisions made under the Act to which its members are subject: the standard expected in the case of appointed representatives is, however, 'with high standards of business conduct'. This probably can be taken as a reference to those of the principles which are applicable. While at first sight this appears less demanding, it should be remembered that, under section 44(6) and (7), the principal is responsible for acts and omissions of the agent within the relevant scope, and is expressly regarded, for the purposes of principles, rules etc, as having committed the acts and omissions of the agent.
[8] *R* v *Lautro, ex parte Ross,* unreported, see *The Times,* 16 January 1991.

CHAPTER 7

CUSTOMER RELATIONS

General

[1] This part of the core rules contains six core rules on:

(a) customer agreements (written 'one way' or 'two way' frameworks for investment services);

(b) customers' rights (exclusion and restriction of liability under the Financial Services Act 1986 or for skill, care and diligence);

(c) suitability (of recommendations and discretionary deals);

(d) standards of advice on packaged products ('best advice');

(e) charges and other remuneration (reasonable in amount and disclosed in advance), and

(f) confirmations and periodic information (deal by deal and periodic accountability).

Customer agreements
(This rule has two paragraphs, treated separately.)

Core rule 14(1)

Where a firm provides investment services to a private customer (other than an indirect customer) on written contractual terms, the agreement must set out in adequate detail the basis on which those services are provided.

Types of customer – private customers
Types of business – all (if written terms)
Type of duty – absolute

[2] **Written customer agreements.** The requirement (that written contractual terms in respect of certain customers must be in an agreement, with certain characteristics) appears to have three separate legal consequences:

(a) If a dispute later arises as to whether particular contractual terms are applicable, there is a need to point to an 'agreement' but no more than an agreement. Written terms of business on the back of documentation, allegedly accepted by conduct, will not suffice unless the result is in truth an agreement. There is, however, no need for any signature, or for all the terms to be in one document, rather than in an exchange of letters or incorporation by reference.

(b) The agreement must set out in adequate detail the basis on which the services are provided. This rule has to be read alongside core rule 9(2) which requires any agreement sent to a private customer to be presented fairly and clearly. To some minor extent the requirements on content overlap with (a) above, since the incorporation by reference of standard contractual terms which are not made available to the counterparty will not satisfy the rule.

(c) As far as the core rule is concerned, there is no need to proceed by way of written agreement, and an oral contract will do, except where core rule 14(2) applies (see below). Even where core rule 14(2) does apply, it does not mean that all services rendered by the firm for that customer have to be under 14(2). A firm can operate with a customer on a written 'two way' agreement for some services, on less formal written agreements under 14(1) for others, and under an oral agreement or arrangement for the rest.

[3] The customers to whom this paragraph relates are private customers who are not indirect customers. So, where Firm A is dealing with Firm B which is acting as agent for its customer C, then, even if Firm A knows that Firm B is acting as agent, Firm A does not have to extend the protection in the paragraph to C, of whose identity and status he may indeed not be aware.

Core rule 14(2)

Where a firm provides to a private customer (other than an indirect customer) investment services involving:

a. contingent liability transactions; or

b. the discretionary management of the customer's assets;

it must do so under a two way customer agreement unless the customer is ordinarily resident outside the United Kingdom and the firm believes on reasonable grounds that he does not wish a two way agreement to be used.

Types of customer – private customers
Types of business – most derivatives; and discretionary management
Type of duty – absolute (but there is one place where belief on reasonable grounds is enough)

Two way customer agreements

[4] A major building block in the 1987 Conduct of Business Rules of the SIB and the SROs etc. was the compulsory customer agreement, together with formal arrangements for content and method of entry, including a requirement to send by post (and various exceptions thereto for the so-called 'impatient customer' etc.). The underlying policy justification appears to have been that,

in the case of a person without substantial experience of investment business, and in circumstances where cancellation rights are not to be made available, there is a need for two elements of investor protection before the customer becomes committed to a relationship (and/or hands over his assets for a purpose) which could involve him in substantial risk. The two elements of consumer protection are, first, that the nature of the services and their potential risks for him should be properly described, and, secondly, he should have an adequate opportunity to consider the terms, without being rushed into an immediate decision then and there.

[5] In the restatement of the core rules, the essence of this policy has been retained, but for a narrower class of business than originally envisaged. The first element of protection is assured because a 'two way' agreement (see the glossary definition) is required, and that involves written form: so core rule 14(1) applies. The second element is also assured because the 'two way' customer agreement is defined in the glossary in a way which imports a duty to be satisfied that the customer has had a proper opportunity to consider the terms of the agreement. Essentially the two way agreement means that there are one or more documents which travel in two directions (either the same document going to and fro, or counterparts, or a lead document and a returned letter or fax etc.) culminating in an assent in writing by the customer. Again, the 'indirect' private customer is excluded.

[6] As to the class of business, a two way agreement is required:

(a) for any transaction in derivatives (or 'ancillaries on them' as provided for by paragraph 3 of the glossary) which will or may make the customer liable to make further payments when the transaction falls to be completed or on closing out: essentially this means margined contracts like futures or written options, or any other derivative with such a propensity for further loss: and

(b) for discretionary management of the customer's assets: while 'investment manager', as used elsewhere in the core rules, includes more than just a discretionary manager, and also covers the manager of a portfolio who has accepted responsibility on a continuous basis for advising on composition, a two way agreement is required only where discretion is conferred upon the manager.

This is a significant relaxation compared with the requirements in the SIB's own conduct of business rules.

[7] There is an exception for customers ordinarily resident outside the United Kingdom who are reasonably believed not to want a two-way agreement: some clients in some countries, it is believed, would not do business in the United Kingdom if they were required to go through this hoop. The firm must, however, believe on reasonable grounds that the customer wishes to waive his right to an agreement in any individual case.

Customers' rights
(This rule has three paragraphs, treated separately.)

Core rule 15(1)

A firm must not, in any written communication or agreement, seek to exclude or restrict any duty or liability to a customer which it has under the Act, or under the regulatory system.

Types of customer – all
Types of business – all
Type of duty – absolute

[8] **Exclusion clauses.** Paragraph 1 prohibits any firm, by contract or by notice ('written communication') from seeking to exclude or restrict duties or liabilities to a customer under the Financial Services Act 1986 or 'the regulatory system'. A duty or liability to a customer under the Act is relatively straightforward: a duty or liability 'under the regulatory system' is defined in the glossary so as to include a duty under rules made by self-regulating organisations. This makes it unnecessary to determine whether SRO rules, which have some status under the Act, do or do not create a duty or liability 'under the Act'. Some of the rules and regulations made by the SIB under the Act already contain provisions which envisage contracting out, or disapplication by written communication. The possibility of exceptions to the duty to segregate client money belonging to a professional or business investor is a good example. In such a case, provided any conditions created by the relevant rules are complied with, the core

rule must be interpreted as not regarding such a provision as creating a duty or liability.

Core rule 15(2)

Similarly, unless it is reasonable to do so in the circumstances, a firm must not, in any written communication or agreement, seek to exclude or restrict:

a. any other duty to act with skill, care and diligence which is owed to a private customer in connection with the provision to him of investment services in the course of regulated business; or

b. any liability owed to a private customer in connection with regulated business for failure to exercise the degree of skill, care and diligence which may reasonably be expected of it in the provision of investment services in the course of that business.

Types of customer – private customers
Types of business – all (regulated business)
Type of duty – not unless reasonable

[9] **Skill, care and diligence: private customers.** Paragraph (2) deals with exclusion or restriction of (further) duties and liabilities on the basis of a reasonableness test. Here the duties and liabilities are those which are owed to private customers, and which are duties (and liabilities for failure) to act with skill, care and diligence. The construction of paragraphs a. and b. is somewhat different, but the purpose appears to have been to produce a similar test for duties and for liabilities alike. The provision is designed to be consistent with the controls over exclusion clauses in the Unfair Contract Terms Act 1977; and to fill, for the benefit of the private customer, a gap left in that Act which contains a general provision disapplying the Act to securities contracts.

Core rule 15(3)

A firm must not seek unreasonably to rely on any provision seeking to exclude or restrict any such duty or liability.

Types of customer – all (paragraph (1)): private customers (in relation to paragraph (2))
Types of business – all
Type of duty – not unreasonably

[10] **Supporting provision relating to the conduct of the firm in the context of complaints.** This paragraph acts as a support to paragraphs (1) and (2), but relates to the operation (rather than formation) of the contract, and to reliance on (rather than giving) the written communication. It requires firms not to behave unreasonably in relying on exclusion clauses etc., and is designed accordingly for two purposes. First it should help to encourage a responsible attitude to complaints and customer redress after a dispute has arisen. Further, it has a transitional operation in that, before the core rules are made to operate in relation to a firm, it may have entered into contracts or given written communications which, when made, were not caught by paragraphs (1) or (2) or otherwise controlled.

Suitability

Core rule 16

(1) A firm must take reasonable steps to ensure that it does not in the course of regulated business or associated business:

a. make any personal recommendation to a private customer of an investment or investment agreement; or

b. effect or arrange a discretionary transaction with or for a private customer or, subject to any exceptions contained in the rules of an SRO of which the firm is a member, any other customer;

unless the recommendation or transaction is suitable for him having regard to the facts disclosed by that customer and other relevant facts about the customer of which the firm is, or reasonably should be, aware.

(2) But where, with the agreement of the customer, a firm has pooled his funds with those of others with a view to taking common management decisions, the firm must instead take reasonable steps to ensure that the transaction is suitable for the fund, having regard to the stated investment objectives of the fund.

Types of customer – private customers (other customers are included in b. but this is subject to exceptions in the SRO's rules)
Types of business – advisory/discretionary
Type of duty – reasonable steps

[11] In the structure built up under the Financial Services Act 1986 for best practice in relation to retail selling, there were three main concepts, 'know your customer', 'suitability' and 'best advice'. This rule deals with the second of those and rule 17 deals with the third. The first, of course, is contained in principle 4 (information about customers) and is referred to in the tailpiece to rule 16(1) as underlying the suitability judgment. In the core rule on suitability, as in the earlier rules, 'suitable' is undefined. There has been much debate as to the level of standard required. The general view is that 'suitability' rests somewhere between the two extremes on the spectrum running from 'not unsuitable' to 'positively and indisputably the most suitable available'. Further, the requirement in the tailpiece to paragraph (1) to have regard to the customer's position connotes that, the more important the transaction is for that customer (e.g. a substantial proportion of his life savings etc.), the more the definition moves to the more exacting end of the spectrum. In its Policy Statement of March 1991 on the 'Regulation of the Marketing of Investment Products and Services', the SIB agreed with the view 'that judgments of suitability have a comparative aspect, so that investment recommendations should not be given without any regard to the merits . . . of alternative types of savings and investment vehicles'. It expected this aspect to be reflected in SRO third tier arrangements.

[12] **Recommendations.** Unlike some of the earlier marketing core rules (e.g. 12 on information about packaged products), suitability is not restricted to purchase recommendations, and operates with equal vigour on other recommendations (whether sales or switches or introductions or agreements for discretionary management services) as long as they relate to an investment or an investment agreement. This wider scope may be relevant in due course in disputes about the suitability of surrender of one life policy and the taking out of another, where there are sometimes suspicions as to whether the consequences in terms of commission for the adviser may have been relevant: here, it should be noted, core rule 26, and 26(2) in particular, has the effect of stressing the suitability requirement, though the test there is 'justified' rather than 'suitable' as such.

[13] **Discretionary transactions.** The second area where suitability applies is in the discretionary management of a portfolio. This is seen as an essential protection in cases where the private customer has placed his trust in the manager. The manager is required to apply the suitability test, in a discretionary portfolio, to every purchase or sale. The paragraph extends beyond the private customer to any other customer, but this is made subject to the exceptions (as defined in the glossary) which SROs may make. At present there are different approaches in the relevant SROs on the question whether suitability requirements should attach to discretionary portfolio management for business and professional investors, that is in the language of the core rules 'non-private customers'.

[14] Paragraph (2) of the rule provides a translation of this in a case where a firm is carrying on collective management 'with the agreement of the customer'. This is effectively a two stage process. Putting the customer into the fund in the first place would normally be caught by paragraph (1) if this was done on a recommendation or in the exercise of discretion. Thereafter, the customer's own personal circumstances become submerged in the fund, and suitability relates to the 'stated investment objectives' of the fund. The combination of the two paragraphs implies some underlying need on the part of the fund manager to identify and state the investment objectives for the fund: for an authorised unit trust, this is in any event required by the SIB's regulations, but something similar seems indicated for other less directly regulated funding systems.

Standards of advice on packaged products
(This rule has six paragraphs, treated separately.)

Core rule 17(1)

A firm which advises private customers to buy packaged products must take reasonable steps to inform itself and relevant agents:

a. where the firm is a product company or its marketing group associate, about packaged products available from the marketing group; or

b. where the firm is an independent intermediary, about packaged products which are generally available on the market and on which it can advise.

Types of customer – private customers
Types of business – advisory/discretionary (on packaged products)
Type of duty – reasonable steps

[15] **Informing oneself and relevant agents about available products.** Rule 17 states the day-to-day part of the polarisation rule, the more structural part having been handled earlier under core rule 4. It requires a two stage process, regulating the anterior search for available products and then the standard of advice at the point of recommendation or use of discretion. In the first stage the rule is general, and in the second stage it operates on a transactional basis, customer by customer.

[16] Polarisation apart, the rule has a major policy impact in the context of 'best advice'. The essence of 'best advice' (whatever the polarity of the adviser) is that a recommendation of a packaged product should not be made unless:

(a) there has been a conscientious search across packaged products available to be recommended, and

(b) the one recommended (except in rare, but important, circumstances: see below) must be believed to be at least as good as any other available.

Paragraph (1) of the rule deals with (a) above, and the remainder of the rule deals with (b).

[17] For the independent adviser, the requirement to search is in paragraph (1)(b) ('must take reasonable steps to inform itself . . . about packaged products which are generally available on the market and on which it can advise'). Generally available connotes available to all, rather than to closed groups only. For the opposite polarity, the equivalent is in paragraph (1)(a) ('must take reasonable steps to inform itself . . . about packaged products available from the marketing group'). The words 'on which it can advise' leave room for the continued development of 'niche-playing' specialist independent financial advisers. Two points need to be noted on this. First, the duty to search, like the rest of the rule, is now limited, for the first time, to persons acting in relation to private customers. The rules about selection of packaged products do not now extend into the area of

the non-private customer. Secondly the paragraph does not cover the discretionary portfolio manager whatever his polarity. Such a manager is subject, in terms of the second stage, to paragraph (3) (if independent) or (2) and (4) (if polarised the other way), and so has to comply with the same standards of selection. At first sight, this may look odd. The answer is, however, that scarcely any independent intermediary will operate only on a discretionary, and not also on an advisory, basis, so paragraph (1) will almost always operate. And paragraph (4) contains the words 'reasonably should be aware' which in practice require tied investment managers to search sensibly if they are going to buy a product outside the group.

Core rule 17(2)-(6)

(2) Where a firm is a product company or its marketing group associate, it must not advise a private customer to buy a packaged product, or buy a packaged product for him in the exercise of discretion, if it is aware of a packaged product of the marketing group which would better meet his needs.

(3) Where a firm is acting as an independent intermediary, it must not advise a private customer to buy a packaged product, or buy a packaged product for him in the exercise of discretion, if it is aware of a generally available packaged product which would better meet his needs.

(4) Where a firm is a product company or its marketing group associate and is acting as an investment manager, it must not advise a private customer to buy a packaged product of a product company outside the marketing group, or buy such a product for him in the exercise of discretion, if it is, or reasonably should be, aware of a generally available packaged product which would better meet his needs.

(5) Where a firm is acting for a private customer as an independent intermediary but not as an investment manager, it must not advise him to buy a packaged product from its extended group if it is aware of a generally available packaged product which is not a product of the extended group and which would meet his needs as well as the extended group product.

> *(6) In assessing the merits of a packaged product to be held as the plan investment of a personal equity plan, a firm must take into account the characteristics (including charging arrangements) of the plan, as well as those of the product.*

Types of customer – private customers
Types of business – advisory and discretionary (on packaged products)
Type of duty – absolute

[18] Paragraphs (2) to (6) deal with the standard of advice itself. The general rule, worked out in detail in the five paragraphs, is that the packaged product recommended must be, as it were, in the 'front rank' of products learned about during the search. 'Is there an available product that would meet the customer's needs better?' is the relevant question.

[19] There is, however, one class of case where the product must not only be in the front rank, but actually ahead of the front rank. This is where the adviser is independent, and is proposing to recommend a packaged product 'from its extended group', that is, broadly, a packaged product which is 'in-house' for any associated company (for the precise detail of this see below). Here, the recommendation may not be made if the 'in-house' packaged product is only in the front rank and therefore not, in the normal language, 'better than best'. The purpose of this particular exception is to make sure that the polarisation rules are not undermined by investment advisers who purport to be independent but who systematically put their customers into the in-house product on the footing that it is as good as any other.

[20] This pattern is worked out in paragraphs (2)-(4) (various aspects of the 'front rank') and paragraph (5) (the 'better than best' exception).

[21] The product company and its marketing associates (those polarised as not independent) must comply:

(a) in all cases, with paragraph (2) (the general 'front rank' rule); and

(b) if the firm is acting as an investment manager additionally with paragraph (4).

Paragraph (2) applies the 'front rank' rule to all the products within the marketing group, whether the firm is advising or acting in the exercise of discretion. Paragraph (4) applies also whenever the firm is advising (or acting in the exercise of discretion) as an investment manager, that is acting under a responsibility to review the portfolio (or with discretion). If in that capacity it is willing to stick to the marketing group products, it can ignore paragraph (4); but if it wishes to go outside the marketing group range, it must then find a product in the 'front rank' of generally available products. This will be relevant to the stockbroker who has his own in-house unit trust company and is polarised on the 'tied' footing to that company. If he is acting as an investment manager, and his 'group' does not deal in life products, he is permitted to recommend etc. in the wider area but subject to paragraph (4). The rule thus treats him almost as if he were independent for that purpose.

[22] The independent intermediary must comply:

(a) in all cases, with paragraph (3) (the general 'front rank' rule); and

(b) if the firm wishes to recommend an 'in-house' product (that is the product of an associated company), additionally with paragraph (5) (the 'better than best' rule described above).

The 'in-house' (or associated) product can be selected only if it is ahead of the front rank. To this, however, there is an exception for the investment manager, that is the manager who has discretionary powers over a fund, or who has accepted responsibility for advising on composition. He may advise in any circumstance on the 'front rank' basis, even if the fund is an 'in-house' (or associated) investment fund. The purpose of this is to assist, for instance, stockbrokers in situations converse to that in paragraph 21 above. Such persons are independent (e.g. because they do not have any in-house insurance products and have chosen to be polarised on the independent side) but may also have an associated unit trust company (the purpose of which is to provide a product to cater inexpensively for the needs of smaller customers). Such investment managers are able to put forward the units in trusts managed by that company without having to demonstrate that those units are superior to any other. They are, under the exception, able to use the associated investment fund if it is as good as any other, without having to show that it is positively better than any other. 'Extended group' is the concept used for associated product companies, and 'group' in this expression means a Companies Act group with the special extension for 'related companies' in paragraph 30 of Schedule 1 to the Financial Services Act 1986. Also included in the 'extended group' are the marketing group associates of any of those members of that Companies Act group.

Charges and other remuneration
(This rule has two paragraphs, treated separately.)

Core rule 18(1)

The amount of a firm's charges to a private customer for the provision of investment services to him must not be unreasonable in the circumstances.

Types of customer – private customers
Types of business – all
Type of duty – not unreasonable

Amount of charges

[23] Paragraph (1) is an apparently simple rule, designed to prevent 'overcharging'. The main area of difficulty in it will be the meaning of 'charges', even with the benefit of the definition in the glossary ('charges' means any charges made to a customer in connection with investment services, including any mark-up or mark-down from the price at which best execution would be achieved). This appears apt to include any charge actually made to a customer, that is a bill presented or deduction made pursuant to an agreement (e.g. a periodical fee for investment management services, a fee for advice or stockbrokers' commission). The reference to mark-up and mark-down also implies that charges include some forms of remuneration, even where their effect is a reduction in the amount of principal paid

over to the customer. It seems, however, that some other forms of remuneration will not be included, such as anything that falls within 'any other remuneration' in paragraph (2). Commission payable by a product company to an adviser or arranger is excluded on this basis, though it falls within the wider ambit of the disclosure rule in paragraph (2).

Core rule 18(2)

Subject to any exceptions contained in the rules of an SRO of which it is a member, before a firm provides investment services to a private customer (other than an indirect customer), it must disclose to him the basis or amount of its charges for the provision of those services and the nature or amount of any other remuneration receivable by it (or, to its knowledge, by its associate) and attributable to them.

Types of customer – private customers
Types of business – all (though SROs can make exceptions)
Type of duty – absolute (though knowledge is relevant in part)

[24] Paragraph (2) deals with disclosure of charges and other remuneration.[1] The dividing line between those two arises in two respects only (see (b) and (c) below): for the most part the rule deals similarly with 'charges for the provision of investment services' and 'any other remuneration attributable to investment services'. The requirements are:

(a) advance disclosure about charges and other remuneration;

(b) for 'charges' the disclosure is of the basis or amount: for 'other remuneration' the disclosure is of the 'nature or amount'. In neither case is the amount necessarily to be disclosed by virtue of the core rule alone. SRO rules may, of course, make more specific requirements in particular circumstances; and

(c) for charges, the person receiving the benefit of the charge is the firm; for other remuneration, there must be disclosure also where the recipient is an associate of the firm and the firm knows about the arrangement.

[25] In relation to discretionary management, or other services supplied pursuant to a customer agreement, it seems sufficient that the disclosure under core rule 19(2) should be made in the customer agreement envisaged by core rule 14. The paragraph is subject to any exceptions contained in the rules of the SRO, which may perhaps relate to matters such as the 'turn' on a principal transaction, the charge made to another customer on an 'agency cross' transaction, or internal charges on a packaged product.

[26] The definitions of inducement and material interest provide a safe harbour for 'disclosable commission on the transaction' from core rules 1 and 2, on broadly the same basis as with soft commission. Only what can genuinely be described as commission receivable in respect of the transaction to the private customer (the word is 'attributable') is protected by the safe harbour. Free holidays etc. would remain vulnerable as inducements, as would 'volume over-riders' which would not be commission of that sort. SRO rules can, however, expand the safe harbour, especially in relation to transactions with non-private customers.

Confirmations and periodic information
(This rule has two paragraphs, treated separately.)

Core rule 19(1)

Subject to any exceptions contained in the rules of an SRO of which it is a member, a firm which effects a sale or purchase of an investment (other than a life policy) with or for a customer must ensure that he is sent with due despatch a note containing the essential details of the transaction.

Types of customers – all
Types of business – all (except life business)
Type of duty – absolute

Contract notes etc.

[27] In one of the broadest provisions in the core rules, paragraph (1) requires any sale or purchase of an investment (except a life policy)

to result in delivery of a note containing the details of the transaction. This extends to principal transactions (see 'with or') and applies wherever there is a customer. Since, however, a customer does not include a market counterparty, the core rule does not require two market counterparties to send to each other equivalent contract notes since neither is a customer of the other.

[28] The heading to the core rule 'confirmations' is a generic phrase. It does not, of course, disturb the existing practice in securities markets of describing the relevant note as a contract note, or that in derivatives markets of describing the relevant note as a 'confirmation note' or difference account: the description of the note in the paragraph itself is apt to cover all documents of this kind. The life policy is excluded because the industry practice in that sector is that the product company accepts the investor's offer, and therefore there is no need for there to be a confirmation as well as the contract documentation.

Core rule 19(2)

Subject to any exceptions contained in the rules of an SRO of which it is a member, a firm which acts as an investment manager for a customer must ensure that he is sent at suitable intervals a report stating the value of the portfolio or account at the beginning and end of the period, its composition at the end, and, in the case of a discretionary portfolio or account, changes in its composition between those dates.

Types of customer – all
Types of business – investment manager
Type of duty – absolute

Periodic reports

[29] The investment manager must send a report at suitable intervals (which will normally be found to be six or twelve monthly if not more often) containing:

(a) the starting value for the period;

(b) the ending value for the period;

(c) the ending composition and

(d) (if discretionary management) intervening changes in composition.

[30] Such a report is of assistance with tax and provides accountability. There is no requirement, at the level of the core rules, for performance comparison, e.g., with a relevant stock market index: this additional accountability is left to the rules of the SRO or to specific agreement between the parties. The requirement applies (except for the fourth point above) to investment managers even if they do not have discretion as such, but have accepted responsibility for advising on composition: these investment managers are given a number of benefits in the core rules as a whole, no doubt on the basis that there would be the accountability, here required, at suitable intervals.

[31] Both paragraphs of the core rule are subject to any exceptions contained in the rules of the SRO.

NOTE

[1] In December 1990, the Secretary of State for Trade and Industry announced his decision on an issue arising in this area from a report of the Director General of Fair Trading: the effect of that decision is that further changes must be introduced within 18 months in the so-called 'disclosure regime'. On this, see further the SIB's April 1991 publication 'Retail Regulation: issues for review'; this indicated at paragraph 7 that the disclosure regime needed further development, since there is still concern that the arrangements are still failing to highlight the essential points and are instead contributing to information overload'. One of the principles to guide the review will be that 'an investor should be made more clearly aware of what kind of product he is buying, what it will cost him, how much of his investment will work for him . . . at all appropriate points in that transaction process' (paragraph 10).

CHAPTER 8

DEALING FOR CUSTOMERS

General

[1] This Part of the Core Conduct of Business Rules contains eight core rules relating to the general aspects of fair dealing on behalf of customers. Among these are two of the most important of all the core rules, from the point of view of the investor: these are 'best execution' which is designed to produce keen pricing in market trading, and 'churning', which is designed to prevent overselling, particularly when the business is driven by commission.

[2] The chapter can be divided into three sub-units as follows:

(a) Core rules 20-25: though drafted in terms of investments as a whole, the general drift of these six core rules relates to fair dealing in the securities and derivatives markets;

(b) Core rule 26 (churning): this relates to over-frequent dealing, mainly of relevance in the investment management and packaged product areas, and

(c) Core rule 27: this relates to derivatives transactions with contingent liabilities only.

Customer order priority

Core rule 20

A firm should deal with customer and own account orders fairly and in due turn.

Types of customer – all
Types of business – dealing firms
Type of duty – fairly and in 'due turn'

[3] The evil at which this core rule is aimed is that of selecting transactions to be done first for some, at the best price, leaving others to get a less satisfactory price. The pre-1991 rule books were considerably more detailed in their requirements here, and the core rule seeks to encapsulate the nature of the requirement by obliging firms to deal 'fairly and in due turn'.

[4] The rule is apt to cover a competition between a customer order and an own account order, and also a competition between two or more customer orders. The ambit of the rule is limited by the meaning given in the glossary to 'order' in relation to an order from a customer: effectively the core rules single out orders where the firm acts as agent or otherwise has the duties of an agent or other fiduciary, and treats these differently from other transactions. So 'net' dealing without agency duties will not be included in the rule. On this see further paragraph 9 below.

[5] It may be expected that more precision may be provided in rules or guidance at the third tier as to what 'in due turn' amounts to in various circumstances. Strict rotation may present practical difficulties and could be unfair when account is taken of transactions of markedly different sizes, but so, too, would be taking any customer substantially out of order without justification. The rule interlocks to some extent with core rule 21.

Timely execution

Core rule 21

(1) Once a firm has agreed or decided in its discretion to effect or arrange a current customer order, it must effect or arrange the execution of the order as soon as reasonably practicable in the circumstances.

(2) But the core rule on timely execution does not preclude a firm from postponing execution of an order where it believes on reasonable grounds that this is in the best interests of the customer.

Types of customer – all
Types of business – effecting and arranging transactions (including discretion)
Type of duty – reasonably practicable

[6] The issue tackled by this core rule is that of delay in carrying out current customer orders, whether that delay is through inefficiency or because of the opportunity sometimes presented by delay in benefiting the firm (or a favourite customer) at the (other) customer's expense. The temptation arises particularly when the firm is dealing as principal. A current customer order, defined in the glossary, includes an order for execution on the fulfilment of a condition (e.g. buy at £1.95) once that condition (viz the market price reaching £1.95) has been fulfilled. The rule covers not only agreements to deal, but decisions on a discretionary basis. In both cases, unswerving compliance with the rule is seen as an important article of faith for dealing firms, and this rule (like its predecessors) is likely to represent a major part of the day-to-day concerns of such firms' compliance officers.

[7] Paragraph (2) permits a departure from paragraph (1) on a 'reasonable belief' basis where it is thought that this is in the best interests of the customer. The classic example will be where he would benefit by postponement of a sell order in a rising market (or the converse), or where immediate dealing in unusually volatile market conditions is judged likely to produce an unfavourable price for the

customer. Another case covered is where aggregation with orders for later execution is seen as reasonable if it would enable a better price to be obtained.

Best execution

Core rule 22

(1) Where a firm deals with or for a private customer, it must provide best execution.

(2) A firm must also provide best execution where it fulfils an order from a non-private customer.

(3) A firm may rely on another person who executes the transaction to provide best execution, but only if it believes on reasonable grounds that he will do so.

(4) For the purposes of the core rule on best execution, a firm provides best execution if:

a. it takes reasonable care to ascertain the price which is the best available for the customer in the relevant market at the time for transactions of the kind and size concerned; and

b. unless the circumstances require it to do otherwise in the interests of the customer, it deals at a price which is no less advantageous to him;

and in applying the core rule on best execution, a firm should leave out of account any charges disclosed to the customer which it or its agent would make.

(5) The core rule on best execution does not require a firm to provide best execution on a purchase of a life policy or on a purchase from the operator of a regulated collective investment scheme of units in the scheme.

Types of customer – private customers; and others where a fiduciary duty is owed

Types of business – dealing firms
Type of duty – 'reasonable care' in ascertaining; absolute in dealing (but with one defence 'if the circumstances require').

[8] This rule relates to one of the most important, and at the same time most difficult, subjects in the securities and derivatives markets. The rule starts with two short paragraphs, laying down the two basic propositions, namely that a private customer must always get best execution, whether the firm deals as principal or as agent: and, secondly, for other customers, best execution must be made available where an 'order' is being fulfilled. The remainder of the rule sets out further ancillary provisions, in particular to define what 'best execution' actually means, in support of these two cardinal points.

[9] As with the core rule 20 on priority, there is a reduction in ambit where the customer is a non-private customer: this results from the use of the phrase 'where it fulfils an order'. As defined in the glossary, an 'order', in relation to an order from a customer, means:

(a) an order to a firm from the customer to effect a transaction as agent;

(b) any other order to a firm from the customer to effect a transaction in circumstances giving rise to similar duties as those arising on an order to effect a transaction as agent;

(c) a decision by a firm in the exercise of discretion for the customer.

[10] This definition therefore seeks to encapsulate the proposition that a duty of best execution is owed whenever the firm is dealing for a non-private customer as agent or in similar circumstances where the fiduciary duties of an agent arise or on a discretionary footing, where the non-private customer has placed his trust in the firm, albeit on a footing of subsequent accountability.

[11] This requirement of best execution runs right across the investment field, apart from the two exceptions set out in paragraph (5), namely purchase of a life policy, and purchase of units in a unit trust etc. from the manager (or other operator). In both these cases, there is, effectively, one supplier only, though a purchase of units in

a unit trust on a market or direct from the existing unit holder will attract best execution if the seller is a firm.

[12] There is no duty of best execution under the core rule if the purchaser is not a 'customer'. Customer is defined among other things as not including a market counterparty, that is a person dealing with the firm as principal (or as agent for an unidentified principal) in the course of investment business of the same description as that in the course of which the firm acts. The market counterparty does not, however, have to be himself authorised. So a New York broker-dealer (not authorised in the United Kingdom) who deals on the London exchange (in reliance on paragraph 26(1) of Schedule 1 to the Financial Services Act 1986) must be given best execution if an order is being fulfilled for him, and if it is apparent that he is dealing as agent for an identified principal. The principal, however, has to be an identified one, not simply one whose existence has been disclosed in an unidentified way. A New York fund manager (who is not doing investment business of the same description as a UK broker-dealer when he deals with him) would be a customer in any event, and entitled to best execution when an order was being fulfilled for him.

[13] What is best execution? The answer is given in paragraph (4), as a two stage operation. The firm must take reasonable care to ascertain the keenest price at the time, and must then deal at a price which is no less advantageous than that. 'No less advantageous' is in the paragraph, because of the frequent practice of ascertaining the best price available and then dealing, as principal, 'at best'. There are important qualifications in a. and b. including conscientious efforts to establish the best price for a transaction of the kind in the relevant market at the time. Relevant 'market' is undefined: as world markets in at least major stocks are becoming steadily more interchangeable and accessible, the reasonable care required will reflect the relevant availability of a market. Paragraph 4(b) also contains words to excuse dealing at a price less advantageous than the keenest price, in circumstances which required the firm to do otherwise in the interests of the customer. Cases where these words will be relevant should be relatively rare, but one example might be where the keenest quotation was from a party that had been known in the past to be unreliable in settlement, and the firm itself had no stock to deal in as principal at that price. In the keenest price, the firm is to leave out of account

charges disclosed to the customer which it or its agent would make. Disclosure of charges is governed by core rule 18, which applies only to the private customer. In other cases, however, core rule 22 assumes that the firm will have reached agreement with or otherwise disclosed to the customer the basis of remuneration. Charges are defined to include mark-up or mark-down from the price at which best execution would be achieved.

[14] Paragraph (3) allows for the transfer to another of the duty to obtain best execution, but only in certain circumstances. These are that the person relied on is the person executing the transaction, and that the firm believes that that person will provide best execution. Since the paragraph uses the word 'person' it is plain that the person relied on may be a foreign dealer not authorised in the UK. If the UK firm has any doubt about delivery of best execution up to UK standards (or better) by the other person, it must take the business elsewhere.

[15] Core rule 22 interlocks in some sense with core rule 3 (soft commission) in that one of the conditions for valid, soft dealing by a firm through a broker on an advisory basis or in the exercise of discretion involves a specific agreement to provide best execution, even if there were no such obligation under core rule 22 itself.

Timely allocation

Core rule 23

A firm must ensure that a transaction it executes is promptly allocated.

Types of customer – all
Types of business – dealing (or 'executing') firms
Type of duty – 'promptly'

[16] The problem to be resolved by this rule is that of late allocation. Allocation of bargains may arise in two cases, one where the only step required is to allocate a bargain to a particular customer (or to the firm), and the other where there is a large deal, whether for purchase

or for sale, which is then broken up into a number of smaller parcels, for one or more customers and/or for the firm itself. This rule applies to both cases. Though the major impact relates to allocations to customers on the one hand and to the firm or its associates on the other, which is where the real mischief could otherwise arise, allocations between favoured and less favoured customers could also be subject to abuse.

[17] In a sense this rule is a variant on late execution (core rule 21), save that the firm (or its employee) tempted to break the rule on timely allocation has the certainty of knowing that the deal has been done and then waits to see which way the market moves in the interim. Requiring prompt allocation should restrain this practice.

Fair allocation

Core rule 24

Where a firm has aggregated an order for a customer transaction with an order for an own account transaction, or with another order for a customer transaction, then in the subsequent allocation:

a. it must not give unfair preference to itself or to any of those for whom it dealt; and

b. if all cannot be satisfied, it must give priority to satisfying orders for customer transactions unless it believes on reasonable grounds that, without its own participation, it would not have been able to effect those orders either on such favourable terms or at all.

Types of customer – all
Types of business – dealing firms
Type of duty – not unfair/reasonable belief

[18] Aggregation has here the special meaning described in the core rule, where orders are bulked together for convenience or for sensible price-related reasons. Where a firm aggregates in this way, and then has to allocate, the basic duty is not to give unfair preference to itself

or to any of the customers. 'Those for whom it dealt' connotes only customers.

[19] The second half of the rule in paragraph b. deals with the case where the aggregated 'buy' (or 'sell') orders are collectively too large for the amount of stock etc. actually obtained (or actually sold). Here the firm must 'give priority to satisfying orders for customer transactions'. On a strict interpretation, this means that 'own account' deals are left out of account until the customers are satisfied. This seems a better reading than the alternative of bringing in the own account orders but giving customers pro rata a somewhat higher percentage of the available stock. There is, however, an exception, rather akin to that in core rule 21(2), on a 'reasonable belief' basis that there are good grounds for giving the firm a pro rata 'slice of the action' even where there is not enough stock to meet orders in full.

Dealing ahead of publications

Core rule 25

Subject to any exceptions contained in the rules of an SRO of which it is a member, where a firm or its associate intends to publish to customers a recommendation or a piece of research or analysis, it must not knowingly effect an own account transaction in the investment concerned or any related investment until the customers for whom the publication was principally intended have had (or are likely to have had) a reasonable opportunity to react to it.

Types of customer – all
Types of business – all
Type of duty – 'not knowingly'

[20] This rule relates to 'front running' of research, a practice clearly described in the core rule itself. The evil is that of publishing a recommendation or piece of research or analysis (typically recommending a share as underpriced or overpriced): the firm then buys (or sells) the stock itself, on the footing that the research or recommendation may be acted upon by customers, the price may then move, and the firm will find itself in possession of a quick profit.

[21] The core rule prohibits the effecting (with knowledge) of an own account transaction in an investment covered by a firm or its associate's potentially price sensitive publication. And the 'pause' required is to give the customers for whom the publication was principally intended a reasonable opportunity to react. While the meaning is relatively plain, the rule contains a substantial number of imprecise concepts, 'publish', 'principally intended' and 'reasonable opportunity' being the main ones. Accordingly, it can be expected that the third tier rules will amplify this provision somewhat, and, indeed, may make a number of exceptions to the rule, in pursuance of the opening words in the rule itself giving power to the SROs to derogate from it.

Churning and switching
(This rule has two paragraphs, treated separately.)

Core rule 26(1)

A firm must not:

a. make a personal recommendation to a private customer to deal; or

b. deal or arrange a deal in the exercise of discretion for any customer;

if the dealing would reasonably be regarded as too frequent in the circumstances.

Types of customer – private customers (recommendation), all (discretion)
Types of business – advisory dealing and discretionary management firms
Type of duty – prohibition if 'reasonably regarded as . . .'.

[22] The evils at which this rule is aimed are those of making recommendations to a private customer to deal too frequently, and dealing on a discretionary basis too frequently for any customer. The underlying purpose, plainly enough, is to stress the need to resist the temptation for reward by transaction-based remuneration, whether

by way of fees, commission or otherwise. The rule applies to personal recommendations (meaning oral or written ones directed to the individual customer) and not to brokers' circulars or other more widely published material. In earlier drafts 'too frequent' was not the only prohibition: 'too large' was also included, but the core rule has now been cut back to cover the whole or at least the latter part of a series rather than a single piece of overenthusiasm. A transaction which was itself too large would normally be caught by the suitability rule (core rule 16).

[23] The thing that is 'too frequent' is the dealing. This is obvious enough in the discretionary case. In the case of a recommendation, the rule tests the immediate recommendation (for 'frequency' purposes) in the context not of frequency of previous recommendations alone but in the context of frequency of dealing, including that which would take place if the immediate recommendation were acted upon. The rule is a rule against loss through persistence, and not against sheer persistence itself.

Core rule 26(2)

A firm must not:

a. make a personal recommendation to a private customer to switch within a packaged product or between packaged products; or

b. effect such a switch in the exercise of discretion for a private customer;

unless it believes on reasonable grounds that the switch is justified from the customer's viewpoint.

Types of customer – private customers
Types of business – advisory and discretionary
Type of duty – absolute unless reasonable belief

[24] Paragraph (2) of this rule imposes a prohibition on a variety of churning, that is 'switching', whether from one packaged product to another or, for example, within a life policy or as between the 'spokes'

of an umbrella fund. The practice of causing an untoward switch from one life policy to another to generate commission is sometimes known as 'twisting' as an alternative word to 'switching'. It is not unknown that the investor's loss in surrender value is greater than the possible benefit he could gain from taking out a new policy. Switching within a life policy relates to unit linked life policies. For umbrella funds the product regulation for authorised unit trusts requires at least one switch a year to be permitted free of charge, and this would presumably be regarded as relevant to the issue of 'justified from the customer's viewpoint'.

Certain derivatives transactions to be on exchange

Core rule 27

A firm must not effect, arrange or recommend a contingent liability transaction with, for or to a private customer unless:

a. the transaction is made on a recognised or designated investment exchange; or

b. the firm believes on reasonable grounds that the purpose of the transaction is to hedge against currency risk involved in a position which the customer holds.

Types of customer - private customers
Types of business - effecting, arranging or recommending (derivatives)
Type of duty - absolute

[25] The lead concept here is the contingent liability transaction; this necessarily involves derivatives and is a successor (more or less) to the earlier concept of 'margined transactions'.[1] Derivative, for this purpose, includes options, futures and contracts for differences (together with ancillaries on them), and, as the glossary shows, the contingent liability in question is one where the contract envisages that a customer 'will or may be liable to make further payments (other than charges and whether or not secured by margin) when the transaction falls to be completed or upon the earlier closing out of his

position'. Some, though not all, derivatives transactions have the characteristic that the amount outlaid at the outset may fall far short of the full amount which the unsuccessful investor could lose. If he purchases an option, the chances are that he will not have to pay more, although, in the event of the market moving against him, his investment could decline to zero. In the case of futures, however, and written options, the prospect of dazzlingly geared-up profit is exactly mirrored by the risk of disastrously geared-up loss.

[26] Accordingly the core rules provide protection for private customers by requiring such transactions to be made on recognised or designated investment exchanges.[2] The purpose of this protection is to ensure that investors who take on contingent liabilities of this kind do not also take on the risk of doing so on an exchange that has not either been recognised by the UK authorities or gone through the process of designation (which includes, among other things, verification of the existence of arrangements for dealing honourably with complaints). Paragraph (b) exempts from this requirement (to trade on exchange for a private customer) hedging transactions against currency risk if the firm reasonably believes that the customer holds a position. This will be so where it actually knows that the customer has a position to be hedged against or where it itself has or had earlier created such a position for him either as principal or as agent and has no reason to suppose it has disappeared.

NOTES

[1] A margined transaction is, generally, a transaction in a future or option where the arrangements on the relevant exchange or otherwise require the payment of margin, that is, a deposit of cash or collateral to secure performance of possible future obligations.

[2] As at 1 April 1991, the recognised and designated exchanges were as follows:

Recognised Investment Exchanges

CME-GLOBEX Chicago Mercantile Exchange (recognised by the Secretary of State)

International Petroleum Exchange of London Ltd

International Stock Exchange of the United Kingdom and the Republic of Ireland Ltd

London Commodity Exchange (1986) Ltd (London FOX) (this includes the former Baltic Futures Exchange)

London International Financial Futures Exchange Ltd
London Metal Exchange Ltd
National Association of Securities Dealers Automated Quotations System (NASDAQ) (recognised by the Secretary of State)
OM London Ltd
Sydney Futures Exchange Ltd (recognised by the Secretary of State)

Designated Investment Exchanges

American Stock Exchange
Amsterdam Port and Potato Terminal Market (NLKKAS- Amsterdam Futures Clearing House)
Association of International Bond Dealers
Australian Stock Exchange
Bourse de Commerce (Lille-Roubaix-Tourcoing)
Bourse de Commerce (Paris)
Chicago Board of Trade
Chicago Board Options Exchange
Chicago Mercantile Exchange
Coffee, Sugar and Cocoa Exchange, Inc
Commodity Exchange, Inc
European Options Exchange
Financiele Termijnmarkt, Amsterdam
Hong Kong Stock Exchange
Irish Futures and Options Exchange (IFOX)
Johannesburg Stock Exchange
Kansas City Board of Trade
Marché à Terme des Instruments Financiers, Paris
Midwest Stock Exchange
Minneapolis Grain Exchange
Montreal Stock Exchange
New York Cotton Exchange (including the Citrus Associates of the New York Cotton Exchange)
New York Futures Exchange
New York Mercantile Exchange
New York Stock Exchange
New Zealand Futures Exchange
Pacific Stock Exchange
Paris Stock Exchange
Philadelphia Board of Trade
Philadelphia Stock Exchange
Singapore International Monetary Exchange
Singapore Stock Exchange

Stockholm Options Market
Sydney Futures Exchange
Tokyo Stock Exchange
Toronto Futures Exchange
Toronto Stock Exchange
Vancouver Stock Exchange

CHAPTER 9

MARKET INTEGRITY

General

[1] This Part of the core rules contains four individual and miscellaneous core conduct of business rules. The common thread running through the four rules is market integrity in that:

(a) insider dealing, often thought of as a fraud on the market, should be further discouraged by the additional civil liabilities imposed through core rule 28;

(b) the practice of stabilisation, strictly controlled under the relevant rules, is generally regarded as defensible in terms of orderly pricing at the outset of an issue or offer for sale, and the relevant SIB rules ensure that customers are warned in any case where such a practice is possible;

(c) it is for the good of market integrity that firms which offer unquoted securities on the basis of two-way prices should be required to ensure that a reasonable repurchase price is available, at least for three months, and

(d) securities bought or sold off-exchange represent a potential problem in terms of subsequent audit and follow-up, with the consequence that orderly arrangements for supply of information concerning such transactions may be required.

Insider dealing
(This rule has three paragraphs, treated separately.)

Core rule 28(1)

A firm must not effect (either in the United Kingdom or elsewhere) an own account transaction when it knows of circumstances which mean that it, its associate, or an employee of either, is prohibited from effecting that transaction by the statutory restrictions on insider dealing.

Types of customer – not relevant (own account transactions)
Types of business – all
Type of duty – absolute, but based on knowledge

[2] Paragraph 1 of this rule provides a civil supplement to the legislation on insider dealing currently in the Company Securities (Insider Dealing) Act 1985. That legislation has two salient characteristics which are relevant here: first, only individuals can be prosecuted for an offence under it; and, secondly, the insider dealing legislation contains no provisions imposing civil liability. The purpose of the legislation, where it deals with civil liability, is not to prevent damages awards, or compensation orders in the criminal courts, but to avoid some of the problems that can arise when securities transactions are annulled, the effect of that on the title conferred by subsequent transactions being only one of the resulting problems. Such difficulties are not, however, attendant upon the creation of civil liability under section 62 of the Financial Services Act 1986, since it is expressly provided there that contravention of rules (including rules made by way of core conduct of business rules) does not invalidate any transaction.[1]

[3] The core rule makes two provisions in support of the criminal statute. Paragraph (1) prevents the firm from effecting an own

account transaction (an expression defined in the glossary) at a time when it knows of circumstances which mean that any individual in its employment or associated with it is prohibited from effecting that transaction by virtue of the insider dealing legislation. So, if any relevant individual in the firm is prohibited, he and any individual with knowledge of the circumstances must avoid effecting any own account transaction for the firm itself in the relevant securities. This accordingly creates civil liability, and in such a way that the firm itself becomes a potential defendant to civil proceedings. The liability arises if the transaction effected is one that the individual was prohibited from effecting, and if the transaction is effected (but not arranged) in the course of investment business or associated business.

[4] This civil effect is enlarged by words in rule 28(1), but substantially narrowed by further words in core rule 36(3). The enlargement is that an own account transaction caught by core rule 28(1) is so caught whether it is entered into in the United Kingdom or elsewhere. So an individual with relevant insider information cannot use a loophole of dealing for the firm on an overseas exchange. On the other hand, the Chinese wall provision in core rule 36(3) should serve to make this potential civil liability manageable. It provides that in a case such as this, which depends upon knowledge, the firm is to be taken to act knowingly only if any of the individuals involved on behalf of the firm acts knowingly. If, therefore, the firm has effective Chinese walls, and the deal was done by persons separated from the persons with inside information by a Chinese wall, civil liability will not arise.

[5] Who are the individuals concerned? Associates are one class, which, for this purpose (individuals only being relevant) will include any individual appointed representative of the firm, or any other person (such as a director or partner) whose business or domestic relationship with the firm or another associate might reasonably be expected to give rise to a community of interest between them which may involve a conflict of interest in dealings with third parties. Employees of the firm or of an associate are another class; they are not defined in the glossary, though 'agent' is defined there as including an employee. The third class of individual is the firm itself, which, plainly, is applicable only to unincorporated sole practitioners.

Core rule 28(2)-(3)

(2) A firm must use its best endeavours to ensure that it does not knowingly effect (either in the course of regulated business or otherwise) a transaction for a customer it knows is so prohibited.

(3) But the core rule on insider dealing does not apply where:

a. the prohibition applies only because of knowledge of the firm's own intentions;

b. the firm is a recognised market maker with obligations to deal in the investment; or

c. the firm is a trustee or personal representative who acts on the advice of a third party appearing to be an appropriate adviser who is not so prohibited.

Types of customer – all
Types of business – all
Type of duty – 'best endeavours'

[6] Paragraph (2) of the rule requires a firm, on a best endeavours basis, not knowingly to effect a transaction for a customer known to be in the same position as an associate or employee in paragraph (1). Such a customer could be an employee or associate of the firm, or another customer. The exclusions from the definition of customer have the effect, however, that the prohibition does not cover, for instance, a market counterparty or a beneficiary under a trust. If a firm deliberately dealt for such a non-customer with knowledge, it would not be in breach of this rule, but might well have a case to answer on principle 1 (integrity).

[7] The rules relating to Chinese walls described above operate so as to limit the scope of knowledge on the part of the firm which is relevant for the purposes of this rule: knowledge appears twice in the provision and core rule 36(3) is apt to cover both references. An example of a case where, even leaving aside the Chinese wall, the

double reference to knowledge could be significant is where the transaction is effected by an appointed representative who does not know of the prohibition, in a case where the firm itself is ignorant of the transaction but well aware that the (unknown) customer is prohibited. Equally, knowledge of one of the two facts could be in the minds of different employees. It is only where the firm can be taken to know both facts that the paragraph has effect.

[8] Paragraph (3) contains three exceptions from both these prohibitions on insider dealing. The first is obvious enough, at least in relation to paragraph (1). If the market sensitive information in question is the knowledge that the firm itself is about to deal, whether for itself or for its customers, it would make no sense to impose a civil prohibition on the firm to prevent it from carrying out that intention. This makes perfect sense in respect of paragraph (1), and appears not to do any major damage to paragraph (2): it will only very rarely occur that a customer who is not an associate or an employee is aware of the firm's own intentions, and that customer would in any event commit a breach of the criminal statute if the deal was effected for him by the firm.

[9] There is also an exception for a firm where it is a recognised market maker with obligations to deal in a way which involves a continuous two way market under the rules of a recognised investment exchange. Recognised market maker for this purpose is defined in the glossary. The purpose of the exception arises from the duty of market makers to make prices. If they were prohibited, on pain of civil sanctions, from continuing to make a price in a security in respect of which they had an obligation to deal, when they had knowledge of inside information, that very fact would itself give a signal to the market. It would also be damaging, in greater or less measure, to market liquidity which depends on an obligation to deal. The limitation of the exception to cases 'where the firm is a recognised market maker with obligations . . .' appears to limit the scope of the exemption, in the case of an integrated house, to the market making arm. In this respect, the core rule appears to be consonant with the exemption from the insider dealing legislation in respect of market makers in section 3(1)(d) of the Company Securities (Insider Dealing) Act 1985. Under that exception knowledge obtained in the course of a business of a market maker does not taint any particular thing done 'in good faith in the course of that business'.

[10] The third exception relates to the trustee or personal representative who obtains, as it were, untainted advice from a third party adviser. Only paragraph (1) of the rule appears in point in this case, since, where the firm is a trustee or personal representative, the beneficiaries are not customers within the meaning of the rules. This exception resolves, at the level of the core rules, a long standing lawyers' conundrum about the position of the trustee who is bound to do the best that he can for his beneficiary, but who is also confronted by the insider dealing legislation. So far as civil liability is concerned, this paragraph entitles him to resolve that conflict in a case where he happens to receive bona fide and apparently independent advice: and the provision draws its roots from an equivalent provision in the Company Securities (Insider Dealing) Act 1985.

Stabilisation of securities

Core rule 29

Where a firm takes action (either in the course of regulated business or otherwise) for the purpose of stabilising the price of securities, it must comply with any applicable provisions of the statutory stabilisation rules.

Types of customer – all
Types of business – any firm taking action for the purpose of stabilising the price of securities
Type of duty – absolute

[11] Stabilisation is a complex subject, best approached through the new criminal offence in section 47(2) of the Financial Services Act 1986. Under this subsection,[2] broadly speaking, intentional price rigging is a criminal offence. During the passage of the Bill for the 1986 Act, concern was expressed that this new criminal offence might have disadvantageous effects on stabilisation practices, as known not only in London and in New York but also in other financial centres. Accordingly, and somewhat unusually, Parliament provided[3] that there would be a defence to section 47(2) for things done for the purpose of stabilising the price of investments if done in conformity with rules made by the SIB. The content of those rules was in part

mandated by Parliament in the 1986 Act or in subsequent amendments.

[12] In the result, therefore, the SIB Conduct of Business Rules contain a special Part[4] devoted to stabilisation. This picks up the specific limitations and definitions in the 1986 Act, and provides a regime for stabilisation of securities. Generally, the most important three features of that part of those rules are:

(a) stabilisation consists of buying or agreeing to buy securities in order to 'prop up' the price following an issue of securities for cash;

(b) the stabilising action is to be taken by one specified 'stabilising manager' and may last only for a maximum of 30 days from the 'closing date' (that is, loosely, the end of the launch); and

(c) relevant documents and announcements have to state that stabilisation is a possibility.

[13] The core rule applies to the stabilising manager referred to at (b) above, and requires him to comply with the SIB stabilisation rules, whether the stabilisation is taking place in the United Kingdom or elsewhere. This international aspect of the subject is apposite because section 47(5), dealing with the territorial aspect of section 47(2), makes the offence depend either on an act done or course of conduct engaged in in the United Kingdom, or on the creation in the United Kingdom of a false or misleading impression. Accordingly, stabilisation overseas in a manner which creates a false or misleading impression in London or Edinburgh etc. can be prosecuted in the British courts. If, however, the stabilising manager has taken action in accordance with the SIB rules, he will have a defence.

[14] The rule applies only to a firm which 'takes action . . . for the purpose of stabilising . . .'. This does not, it seems, include other firms who are aware that stabilising action may be or has been taken by others and who are required to make appropriate disclosures in accordance with limb (c) at paragraph 12 above. Those disclosures may be those set out in the SIB rules themselves: but the rule does not specifically look through to the SIB stabilisation rules in this respect, and this aspect of the subject is likely to be regulated by the special rules for the purpose made by the relevant self-regulating organisa-

tion/s. Those rules will, in part, no doubt be made in support of core rule 10 (customers' understanding) because of the clear risk to a customer of buying a security whose price is being supported for a brief introductory period. In part, however, the supporting rules may relate to core rule 29, because of the systemic issues relating to market integrity in the context of statutory stabilisation. The SIB's rules in chapter 10 cover both aspects.

[15] In practice, firms close to the actual stabilisation (such as those which have chosen the stabilising manager to act for all of them as required by the SIB rules) may find it sensible to follow the SIB stabilisation disclosure regime (even if they are members of a relevant SRO). This would be because there is a possibility (not yet tested in the courts) that they might then themselves benefit from the statutory defence in section 48(7), even though, like the core rule, it is expressed as limited to 'anything done for the purpose of stabilising the price of investments'.

Off-exchange market makers

Core rule 30

Where a firm sells to a private customer any securities which are not quoted on a recognised or designated investment exchange, whilst giving the customer the impression that the firm is a market maker in the investment concerned, it must:

a. give notice to the customer that it is required to ensure that a reasonable price for repurchase of the investment is available to him for a specified period which must not be less than three months after the date the notice is given; and

b. ensure that such a price is available to him for that specified period.

Types of customer – private customers
Types of business – dealing firms
Type of duty – absolute

[16] This rule is concerned with the firm's selling of unlisted securities to private customers on the basis that the customer might

expect that the firm would buy them back if necessary. Some years ago, there were a substantial number of 'off-exchange market makers' (that is, persons whose business it was to do deals of this kind), but the changes in regulation, in economic circumstances and in other technological and commercial developments have made them now much rarer than they were.

[17] Nonetheless, the core rule provides a basic right to the customer; he can reverse his transaction during a period of (at least) three months from the sale at a reasonable price, and he has to be informed of that right. The duty to make available a reasonable price does not mean a warranty that the securities will continue to have at least the same value as on sale, nor, presumably, does it require a price to be offered at greater than a reasonable value. Nonetheless, the core rule provides some assurance to private customers dealing with such firms that the unquoted securities which they are offered are being and will be offered on a two way basis. The amount of the then selling price, if there still was one, would obviously be relevant to the reasonableness of the repurchase price made available.

Reportable transactions

Core rule 31

Unless otherwise provided by the rules of an SRO of which it is a member, a firm must make available to its regulator details about transactions (including own account transactions) in securities which it effects other than on a recognised investment exchange.

Types of customer – all
Types of business – firms dealing in securities
Type of duty – absolute

[18] This rule relates to transaction reporting and the context, for reasons which follow, is that of off-exchange securities transactions, that is, where an authorised person deals privately with another person or where the deal is done on an exchange which is not recognised for the purpose in the UK. The underlying purpose is that regulators need in appropriate cases to be satisfied that there is being maintained an effective audit trail, that is to follow relevant

transactions sequentially into, within and out of the firm concerned in order to be sure about, for instance, compliance with best execution obligations and other aspects of propriety in dealings.

[19] Where the exchange is a recognised investment exchange,[5] the regulator may assume that the exchange will be able to assist with an audit enquiry of this kind. Under Schedule 4 to the 1986 Act, such an exchange must either itself have or secure the provision on its behalf of satisfactory arrangements (that is arrangements satisfactory to the SIB, or, if the exchange is an overseas exchange, to the Secretary of State) for recording the transactions effected on the exchange. It also needs to have effective arrangements for the investigation of complaints in respect of business transacted by means of its facilities, and must be able to cooperate, by the sharing of information and otherwise, with other persons concerned, including SRO regulators.

[20] The rule is imprecise on the question whether the information must be kept by the firm and made available to the regulator only on demand, or whether there has to be a routine supply of information. Matters of this kind can be expected to be dealt with by the individual SRO regulators. They also have a power by rules to make other provision, including power to disapply the rule to their members in whole or in part. This rule is the only rule among the 40 which can be wholly disapplied by the SROs in the third tier.

NOTES

[1] See section 62(4), final proposition.
[2] Section 47(2) reads – 'Any person who does any act or engages in any course of conduct which creates a false or misleading impression as to the market in or the price or value of any investments is guilty of an offence if he does so for the purpose of creating that impression and of thereby inducing another person to acquire, dispose of, subscribe for or underwrite those investments or to refrain from doing so or to exercise, or refrain from exercising, any rights conferred by those investments.'
[3] Section 48(7), (7A), (8) and (9): not set out in this book.
[4] Part 10 of the Financial Services (Conduct of Business) Rules 1990: not set out in this book.
[5] For a list of recognised investment changes see the first part of the list at chapter 8 note 2.

CHAPTER 10

ADMINISTRATION

[1] Under this heading are grouped six core rules relating to general matters affecting the firm's administration. As these rules are general, all of them except one (rule 37 – cessation of business), apply whoever the customer is. Matters of administration tend to be arranged for the firm as a whole, rather than just in relation to specific types of customer. This heading contains the first of two core rules which, rather than imposing obligations on firms, provide them with benefits (variously thought of as 'safe harbours', 'comfort' or, in legal language, defences): this is core rule 36 on Chinese walls.

Safeguarding of customer investments

> **Core rule 32**
>
> A firm which has custody of a customer's investments in connection with or with a view to regulated business must, subject to any exceptions contained in the rules of an SRO of which it is a member:
>
> a. keep safe, or arrange for the safekeeping of, any documents of title relating to them;
>
> b. ensure that any registrable investments which it buys or holds for a customer in the course of regulated business are properly registered

in his name or, with the consent of the customer, in the name of an eligible nominee; and

c. where title to investments is recorded electronically, ensure that customer entitlements are separately identifiable from those of the firm in the records of the person maintaining records of entitlement.

Types of customer – all
Types of business – any firm with custody of a customer's investments (in connection etc. with regulated business)
Type of duty – absolute

[2] This rule provides an overview of the general duties of a custodian of investments. The context is that of documents of title (or their electronic equivalent) including registered title. Clients' money, another asset within principle 7 (customer assets) does not appear within the core conduct of business rules: see further Part D below.

[3] The most general of the three obligations is to keep safe or arrange for the safekeeping of documents of title. Where the firm elects to keep the documents itself, the liability remains with it. Where it elects to employ an agent, there is room for argument as to whether the duty to 'arrange for the safekeeping' involves the retention of or transfer of responsibility. The better view, coupled with the underlying law on wrongful interference with goods, suggests that the liability remains with the firm.

[4] The second duty relates to registrable investments. These, if bought or held for a customer, must be properly registered in the name of the customer or, if he consents, in one of the three classes of eligible nominee in the glossary: these are individual nominees, broadly speaking, at arm's length from the firm, and chosen by the customer; a corporate nominee with no other business, or an institution authorised under the Banking Act 1987. Where the core rule requires the corporate nominee to have no other business this means no other distinct business: the normal activities of a nominee company such as paying over dividends etc. are included.

[5] The third obligation concerns electronic recording of title to investments, and covers existing systems of this kind as well as

looking forward to the TAURUS system expected to be introduced in 1992 by the International Stock Exchange, following enabling legislation in the Companies Act 1989. The basic obligation here is that the entitlement of the customer must be separately identifiable from the entitlements of the firm, at least in the records of entitlement. In this respect this requirement reflects principle 7 (customer assets) which requires a firm to arrange proper protection ‘by way of segregation and identification of those assets or otherwise’.

[6] Since custody services of themselves are not authorisable activities, the scope of the rule is related to custody services ‘in connection with or with a view to regulated business’. This particular form of words for envisaging a link of some kind with investment business is unique in the core rules, though ‘in connection with’ is the same phrase as is used in ‘associated business’. Requirement (b), however, has the additional restriction that registrable investments held in custody are only those which are bought or held ‘in the course of regulated business’.

[7] The purpose of the link with investment business is best understood in terms of *vires*. The SIB’s powers to regulate business have to have some connection with investment business; the precise limits are explored in more detail in chapter 11 in relation to core rule 40. So this core rule governs custody of, for instance, share certificates or other documents of title to securities following or with a view to investment business. But separate safe custody services in relation to share certificates etc., for example of a bank, are not included if the bank has and has had nothing to do with acquisition, or management or possible disposal. This is the case even if the bank is an authorised person.

Scope of business

Core rule 33

A firm must maintain a business profile describing the kind of investment business it carries on in the United Kingdom and may carry on (and hold itself out as carrying on) investment business in the United Kingdom of that kind only.

Types of customer – not relevant: rule relates to business
Types of business – all
Type of duty – absolute

[8] There are two requirements here. First is the requirement to maintain a business profile. Strictly this is an undefined expression, but the core rule itself provides the context and purpose: the business profile must describe the kind of investment business carried on in the United Kingdom. The second duty is that the firm must keep within the scope set out in that profile. In other words, if the firm's profile does not extend to investments of a particular kind (e.g. derivatives) or states that it does not handle client money, the rule is broken if the profile is exceeded. A subsidiary element in the second of these requirements, but one which has proved extremely important in the early years of regulation, is that the firm may not hold itself out as carrying on business outside the scope of that profile. So choosing an investment firm because of what it says it can and cannot provide is based on solid regulatory backing, and loss caused to an investor if the firm goes beyond its limits is recoverable.

[9] In the case of members of SROs, the third tier requirements, like their predecessors, are likely to require that the profile be agreed with the SRO. So initial scope and changes in scope will require the consent of the regulator. In the case of directly regulated bodies, the position is not on all fours, since the SIB's powers do not extend to requiring firms to agree a profile with it. Nonetheless a business plan is required and is to be notified to and is frequently discussed with the SIB as direct regulator because of the powers of intervention that are available if the SIB is not content with an enlargement of scope.

[10] The scope involved in the business profile will customarily cover different sectors of the business, such as futures and options, packaged products, business expansion schemes etc. The rule is, however, wide and flexible enough to be able to treat 'investment business not involving the holding of client money' as a kind of investment business, and there is room for some variation in practice, accordingly, at least as far as this core rule is concerned. The individual regulators tend to have their own separate approaches to the practice under this general rule.

Compliance

Core rule 34

(1) A firm must take reasonable steps, including the establishment and maintenance of procedures, to ensure that its officers and employees and officers and employees of its appointed representatives act in conformity with:

a. their own and their employer's relevant responsibilities under the regulatory system;

b. where relevant, the requirements of the statutory restrictions on insider dealing; and

c. appropriate arrangements on propriety in personal dealings.

(2) A firm must take reasonable steps, including the establishment and maintenance of procedures, to ensure that sufficient information is recorded and retained about its regulated business and compliance with the regulatory system.

(3) Records required to be maintained by the regulatory system may be inspected by a person appointed for the purpose by the firm's regulator.

Types of customer – not relevant, rule relates to firms as a whole
Types of business – all
Type of duty – absolute

[11] Building on and providing more detail than principle 9 (internal organisation), this rule provides, on a reasonable steps basis, for the establishment of compliance systems to ensure that there is conformity with the three general areas described, that is the regulatory system itself, insider dealing, and 'propriety in personal dealings'. A number of the regulatory bodies have established standards for a firm's compliance. These have various titles and differ somewhat in points of detail, but the overall concentration is firmly on the requirement of the firm, including its structure, administra-

tion, personnel systems and procedures, to secure compliance on a systematic, organised and ethical basis.[1]

Complaints

Core rule 35

(1) A firm must have procedures to ensure:

a. the proper handling of complaints from customers relevant to its compliance with the regulatory system;

b. that any appropriate remedial action on those complaints is promptly taken; and

c. where the complaint is not promptly remedied, that the customer is advised of any further avenue for complaint available to him under the regulatory system.

(2) A firm must cooperate with a person appointed by its regulator to investigate complaints.

Types of customer – all
Types of business – all
Type of duty – absolute

[12] This rule deals with the general topic of consumer redress, though the language used is that of 'complaint' and 'remedial action'. The coverage is in respect of anything relevant to the firm's compliance with the regulatory system, that is the arrangements for regulating a firm under the Act, including the Principles, the Core Conduct of Business Rules and the rules of the firm's regulator. The basic standards set out, and required to be in a procedure, are proper handling, prompt remedial action on the complaints and advice as to further recourse if a prompt remedy is not forthcoming. In a further provision, the firm is required to cooperate with a person appointed by the regulator as an investigator of complaints. While the firm is not thereby obliged to accept the recommendation or 'finding' of a complaints investigator, the duty to assist in the process is a useful

step towards sensible arrangements for dispute resolution, at the levels of the firm and of the regulator alike.

Chinese walls

Core rule 36

(1) Where a firm maintains an established arrangement which requires information obtained by the firm in the course of carrying on one part of its business of any kind to be withheld in certain circumstances from persons with whom it deals in the course of carrying on another part of its business of any kind, then in those circumstances:

a. that information may be so withheld; and

b. for that purpose, persons employed in the first part may withhold information from those employed in the second;
but only to the extent that the business of one of those parts involves investment business or associated business.

(2) Information may also be withheld where this is required by an established arrangement between different parts of the business (of any kind) of a group, but this provision does not affect any requirement to transmit information which may arise apart from the Core Conduct of Business Rules.

(3) Where the Core Conduct of Business Rules apply only if a firm acts with knowledge, the firm is not for the purposes of the Core Conduct of Business Rules to be taken to act with knowledge if none of the relevant individuals involved on behalf of the firm acts with knowledge.

(4) In addition, in order to avoid the attribution of information held within a firm to that firm for the purposes of section 47 of the Act, the effect of section 48(6) of the Act is that nothing done in conformity with paragraph (1) of the core rule on Chinese walls is to be regarded as a contravention of section 47 of the Act.

Types of customer – not relevant
Types of business – all
Type of duty – not relevant

[13] This rule deals with the general subject of the Chinese wall as defined in paragraph (1) ('an established arrangement . . .'); effectively, it confers a number of defences on firms which they would or might otherwise not have had available to them. One element of the 'Big Bang' as it took place in the London securities markets, and elsewhere in the United Kingdom, was the arrival of multiple capacity investment houses. The problems about confidentiality of information as between different arms of such an integrated house was soon diagnosed as a problem requiring attention, and the Chinese wall was the response to the need for a workable system that would not expose firms to undue liability on the basis of knowledge attributed across from one part of the firm to another in accordance with traditional legal doctrine. Parliament acknowledged the existence of this problem, and referred to the desirability of Chinese walls, in at least two places in the Financial Services Act 1986.[2] Tracking one of these, paragraph (1) of the core rule describes the Chinese wall as 'an established arrangement which requires information obtained by the firm in . . . one part of its business to be withheld in certain circumstances from persons with whom it deals in . . . another part of its business'. As long as at least one of those parts is involved in investment business or 'associated business' (business carried on in connection with investment business, such as principal or own account deals), the paragraph permits information to be withheld from the persons with whom it deals. There is, thus, an approved justification for not supplying information which otherwise would or might have to be supplied.

[14] The paragraph goes on to deal with the withholding of information not in relation to persons with whom the firm deals (whether technically customers or not), but the withholding of information from employees on the other side of the wall. This permission to withhold from the employees is, however, not a free-standing or independent matter, but one that is dependent upon the primary purpose of the rule, namely the use of the Chinese wall in relation to information withheld from customers etc.

[15] The provision is designed to attract, among other things, the specific defence in the Financial Services Act 1986, section 48(6): under that subsection, Parliament accepted that where the SIB made rules relating to Chinese walls, nothing done in conformity with those rules should be regarded as a contravention of section 47 (misleading

statements and practices). Only the SIB's rules attract the benefit of that subsection, and that is one of the principal reasons for the existence of the rule on Chinese walls in core rule form.

[16] Paragraph (2) deals with a similar issue, not as between different parts of a business, but as between different parts of the business of a group. Insofar as it might be thought, in relation to an obligation imposed by the core conduct of business rules, that information contained in one company in a group should be transmitted to another, the paragraph reverses that proposition. But it is careful to do so in a way which leaves the outlying law, including section 47, unaffected in this respect.

[17] Paragraph (3) offers a further supporting protection, in relation to those of the core conduct of business rules which depend upon knowledge on the part of the firm. Good examples of such core rules are 25 (dealing ahead of publications) and 28(1) and (2) (insider dealing). Core rule 36(3) gives the firm a defence in relation to any such obligation if none of the relevant individuals involved had the requisite knowledge.

[18] Paragraph (4) states some of the propositions discussed above, but does not itself have any legislative effect beyond acting as an explanation.

Cessation of business

Core rule 37

(1) Where a firm or its appointed representative decides to withdraw from providing any investment or related custodian services to private customers, the firm must ensure that any such business which is outstanding is properly completed or is transferred to another firm.

(2) Where the interests of private customers of a firm would be significantly affected by the death or incapacity of an individual within the firm, the firm must make arrangements to protect the interests of those customers in that event.

Types of customer – private customers
Types of business – all
Type of duty – absolute

[19] This rule seeks to mitigate the irritation and risk to private customers where a firm decides to withdraw from any particular class of services leaving outstanding transactions uncompleted: and it also covers the equivalent problem of exposure of private customers to the risk of loss of a particular individual within the firm, perhaps someone with irreplaceable knowledge or experience.

[20] The requirement, in the former case, is to ensure that outstanding business is properly completed or else transferred to another firm. The requirement for the second is that the firm must make arrangements to protect the interests of private customers whose interests would be significantly affected by the death or incapacity of an individual within the firm. This part of the core rule is less specific, no doubt because the circumstances are more variable than in the case of incomplete transactions. A sole practitioner, for instance, confronts different problems in complying with rule 37(2) from those faced by a medium size or large firm with one or two particularly gifted or critically important staff members.

NOTES

[1] See, for instance,:

(a) The Securities Association: 'Standards for Compliance with Regulatory Requirements' (March 1990);

(b) IMRO: 'Compliance Standards and the Compliance Function' (June 1990);

(c) The Chartered Association of Certified Accountants 'Professional Standards and Guidelines for Compliance Officers' (December 1990).

[2] Section 48(2)(h) and 48(6).

CHAPTER 11

GENERAL

[1] Introductory. This set of three remaining core rules contains no further obligations. Core rule 38 offers various alleviations and 'safe harbours' particularly when the person concerned is acting in conformity with guidance received, or is acting in reliance on information received. Core rule 39 gives SROs the ability to adjust the border between the private customer and the non-private customer in the special circumstances set out in the core rule. And core rule 40 deals, at considerable length, with the method of application of the remainder: questions such as territorial scope, particular disapplications for specific classes of business and specific types of advertisements are all included.

Reliance on others

Core rule 38

(1) A person is to be taken to act in conformity with the Core Conduct of Business Rules to the extent that:

a. the relevant regulator has issued formal guidance on compliance with them; and

b. in reliance on standards set in that guidance, the person concerned believes on reasonable grounds that he is acting in conformity with the rules.

(2) A person is to be taken to act in conformity with any of the Core Conduct of Business Rules as to information, to the extent that he can show that he reasonably relied on information provided to him in writing by a third party whom he believed on reasonable grounds to be independent and competent to provide the information.

(3) Any communication required under the Core Conduct of Business Rules to be sent to a customer may be sent to the order of the customer, so long as the recipient is independent of the firm; and there is no need for a firm to send a communication itself where it believes on reasonable grounds that this has been or will be supplied direct by another person.

Reliance on guidance

[2] The core rules are at an intermediate level of generality, and are deliberately not wholly precise in prescribing the detailed conduct required. Indeed, some of the press comment on the rules has described them as the '39 reasonable steps'. Accordingly, it may be expected that some of the rules, though perhaps not all, may need detailed support to spell out what is required. Some of the discussion of particular rules (above) has mentioned this aspect.

[3] Core rule 38 offers special legal results to the SRO regulators who provide supporting detail (as they think required) in the form of guidance. This may be of advantage in that guidance, unlike third tier rules, does not create fresh obligations, but can spell out what the obligation in the core rule itself entails. The purpose of paragraph (1) therefore is to enable firms to have some comfort that, if they comply with the SRO's guidance, they do not incur the risk of proceedings for allegations of breach, whether in court or in a disciplinary forum.

[4] The rule has three conditions relating to the guidance itself, and two relating to the person's own position. The guidance must be 'formal guidance', it must relate in some way to compliance with the core rules, and it must set standards. Formal guidance will be guidance of a character that falls within the Financial Services Act 1986 section 8(4), or, in the case of the SIB as a regulator, section 114(12). Guidance of this character attracts

the 'competition proofing' arrangements set out in, for instance, section 120(4) or section 121(2): if the guidance appears to the Secretary of State, on the advice of the Director General of Fair Trading, to have or to be intended to have an adverse effect on competition, he has powers to direct that that defect be remedied.

[5] Secondly, the guidance has to be guidance on compliance with the core rules, either generally or individually. Impliedly, therefore, this means guidance issued after 30 January 1991, and after or in contemplation of the commencement order in respect of the relevant SRO.

[6] Thirdly the guidance must be guidance which sets standards. This will be particularly relevant for subjective and other judgmental expressions in the core rules including 'fairly', 'promptly', 'adequate detail' etc. It is also apt for situations where the SRO spells out the steps required to comply with the core rule in other circumstances. But, if the guidance were to deal with interpretation of the legal requirements, or to set out factual circumstances on which the firm relied (e.g. whether or not a particular exchange was recognised or designated), the legal effect of core rule 38(1) would not be available.

[7] The person concerned has also to satisfy two further requirements in order to benefit from the safe harbour of the paragraph. He must rely on standards set in the guidance, and he must believe on reasonable grounds that he is acting in conformity with the relevant rules.

Reliance on independent information.

[8] Paragraph (2) deals with reliance on information provided to a person by a competent and independent third party. This protection is given where the reliance on such a third party was reasonable and is available for any core rule on information. The requirement for independence will usually mean that the paragraph does not figure in cases of product information etc. supplied by product providers, though paragraph (3) of the core rule may be of assistance there. A good example of reliance under core rule 38(2) is in respect of 'the buying process' in rule 11(2). When advising a private customer to buy a packaged product, the firm must take reasonable steps to

ensure that the customer is given adequate information about the buying process: this is a reference to the so-called Buyer's Guide, set out by the regulators: and so using the relevant regulator's documentation, even if not required but merely recommended, in guidance would be good enough for that part of core rule 11(2).

[9] The first part of paragraph (3) deals with communications being sent not to the customer himself but to his order. So long as the nominee is independent of the firm, sending communications to the nominee is equivalent (for the purposes of the core rules) to sending them to the customer himself. The firm obliged to send a notice or other communication is entitled not to do so in cases where it reasonably believes that a third person has supplied or will supply the material, e.g. product particulars.

Core rule 39: Classes of customer
(For the text of this core rule, see annex 2.)

[10] As discussed in chapter 4, the core rules divide the customers into two classes, private and non-private. Core rule 39 recognises, however, that this split may prove to be inadequately sophisticated to deal with a possible intermediate class, known in the previous rule books as the 'experienced investor'. So core rule 39 is, in substance, an enabling provision permitting SRO rules to treat someone on the private customer side of the line as if he were on the other side of it. To achieve this effect, the SRO rules would need to comply with conditions a. to c. in the core rule, basing themselves on a reasonable belief that the customer has sufficient experience and understanding to waive the protections provided for, has been warned in writing, and clearly, about the loss of protection and, after a proper opportunity to consider that warning, has consented in writing.

[11] This requirement of a proper opportunity to consider the warning is drafted in a manner strikingly similar to the 'two way customer agreement', that is where the firm has to believe on reasonable grounds that the customer has had a proper opportunity to consider the terms of the agreement, except that the rule 39(1) c. phrasing goes directly for 'a proper opportunity' not what the firm is satisfied is a proper opportunity. Even so, in appropriate cases, these two steps can perhaps be combined. As to 'waiving the protections' the test of sufficient experience and understanding appears to denote

that the customer knows what he is doing when he gives up his rights. A possible (but unlikely) alternative construction would be that he had sufficient experience and understanding of the investment world to be 'justified in waiving' the protections. Either way, the rules cannot validly enable the waiver to take place except after some reasonably thorough consideration of the experience and understanding of the customer, and the burden of proof is on the firm.

[12] Paragraph (2) enables the SRO rules to dispense with written consent for customers ordinarily resident outside the United Kingdom who do not wish to consent in writing. It is understood that there are some countries in the world where written agreements of this sort can pose real problems for customers, whether on religious or on political grounds or both. Again the comparison with core rule 14(2) is close.

Core rule 40: Application of the Core Conduct of Business Rules
(For the text of this core rule, see annex 2.)

[13] The main effect of this rule has been described in outline in chapter 4. It divides into four substantial paragraphs, relating to rules of application for business, rules of application for advertisements, rules of application as to time, and interpretation. The most complicated of these (and the only one tackled in chapter 4 above) is the first.

[14] Before considering the various rules about business in core rule 40, it may be convenient to establish a number of concepts relating to business, as follows:

(a) 'investment business': this is defined in section 1 of the Financial Services Act 1986 by reference to Schedule 1 to that Act; investment business is subdivided for the core rules into two subsets, that is:

(i) 'regulated business' (see below) and

(ii) 'investment business which is not regulated business';

(b) 'investment services': this is defined, in the glossary, as activities undertaken in the course of carrying on investment business;

(c) 'regulated business' (also defined in the glossary) means, loosely speaking, investment business in the UK, though the reader will need to look out for the fine print in the glossary (see further paragraph 16 below).

(d) 'associated business' (also defined in the glossary) is business carried on in connection with investment business: some of the possible connections are specified in the core rules (e.g. custody services in core rule 32) while others will depend upon the individual facts.

(e) 'business held out as being for the purposes of investment': apart from the reference in rule 40(1) b., this is never specifically referred to as such in the core rules, but is brought in by inference in a number of the core rules, such as 28(2) (which contains the words 'or otherwise'). Its origin, plainly enough, is in section 48(4) of the Financial Services Act 1986.

[15] Rules referring to investment services look through to the underlying investment business, and therefore are clad in the same clothes, so far as scope is concerned, as if they had referred to 'business' not 'services'.

[16] Where 'associated business' is included, it will be so included to the extent that the investment business with which it is connected is included. So if the rule concerned is limited to regulated business, associated business will be included only if connected to regulated business. The same will be true of 'business held out as being for the purposes of investment'.

[17] A number of the core rules do not relate to business at all, but to the constitution and internal management of the firm. Examples of this are rules 13 (appointed representatives), 34 (compliance) and 35 (complaints). These all have their own separate borderlines, in that rule 13 is itself bounded by the scope for use of appointed representatives in section 44 of the Act, and also contains a reference to regulated business and to 'financial business' (see the glossary) in paragraph (3). Rules 34 and 35 take as their general boundary 'the regulatory system' as defined in the glossary.

[18] Regulated business is a topic of some complexity at the edges, though the basic content (see paragraph 14 above) is plain. If the firm has a base in the UK all investment business carried on from that base is covered. This will be so even if the firm has its place of incorporation overseas. If the firm is operating from a base overseas, the investment business done from there will (subject to two exceptions) be regulated business if carried on with or for customers in the UK. This is the basic outcome. The definition also provides that to be regulated business, business from a UK base does not have to be for a customer (whether in the UK or elsewhere): this is different from the equivalent for business from a foreign base, which has to be for a customer and for one who is in the United Kingdom. Secondly, even business for a UK customer from the foreign base is not regulated business if it comes from a branch and 'would not be treated as carried on in the United Kingdom if that [branch] were a separate person'. This has the effect of enabling foreign branches to treat as unregulated business anything which could have been lawfully carried on in the United Kingdom without requiring authorisation, because of the special 'permitted import' rules in paragraphs 26 and 27 of Schedule 1 to the Financial Services Act 1986. There is an equivalent exception for the foreign business of an appointed representative.

[19] In one rule (33) the phrase 'investment business in the United Kingdom' is used. In many cases this will mean 'regulated business', though circumstances can be imagined when not all regulated business (and indeed some investment business which is not regulated business) would be 'investment business in the United Kingdom'. The reason for this unique reference is that rule 33 is concerned with an obligation on the firm to state what can be done in the UK, and then to do that only. So the more normal subdivisions of investment business into regulated and unregulated would not fit that special circumstance.

Index of application of core rules

[20] It may help to list the core rules and give a broad indication of their application in terms of business etc. The following list takes as the main concepts the following:

A investment business

B that part of investment business which is 'regulated business'

C that part of investment business which is not 'regulated business'

D 'associated business'

E business which is held out as being for the purposes of investment

F 'own account transactions' (these will feature, as appropriate, in one or more of B, C or D).

It will be seen that the most frequent application is B (regulated business), with the others being departures from that pattern for special reasons. Where a rule has two different scopes, for different paragraphs, both are signalled.

1. B or 'otherwise' if there is a conflict with duties owed in B.
2. B
3. B
4. B
5. Advertisement: see core rule 40(2)a.
6. Advertisement: see core rule 40(2)a.
7. C/B
8. C
9. B (see paragraph 15 above)
10. B
11. B (see paragraph 15 above)/B
12. B
13. Firm as a whole (see paragraph 17 above)
14. B (see paragraph 15 above)
15. ADE/B
16. BD
17. B
18. B (see paragraph 15 above)
19. B
20. BF
21. B
22. B

23. B
24. BF
25. F
26. B
27. B
28. F(UK or elsewhere)/ADE ('or otherwise')
29. ADE ('or otherwise')
30. B
31. BF
32. D or with a view to B
33. A in the United Kingdom (see paragraph 19 above)
34. See paragraph 17 above
35. See paragraph 17 above
36. AD
37. BD
38. No special scope
39. No special scope
40. Governs scope of other rules

[21] Sub-paragraphs c. to f. of core rule 40(1) deal with special cases of disapplication, including powers to disapply. Sub-paragraph c. deals with the recognised professional bodies and exempted persons. The first of these states a consequence of the primary legislation, while the second repeats the 'shut-out' already in the relevant rule books for business done pursuant to an exemption in sections 42-46. Sub paragraph d. repeats the legal consequence of partial power to regulate concerning insurance companies, friendly societies and UCITS[1] operators and trustees.

[22] Sub-paragraphs e. and f. give power to the relevant SROs (in practice the Securities and Futures Authority and the Financial Intermediaries Managers and Brokers Regulatory Association, FIMBRA) to make exceptions of a general character for oil market participants investing in the Brent Market etc. and for publishers giving investment advice.

Advertisements

[23] Paragraph (2) of rule 40 provides special rules for application for advertisements. Sub-paragraph a. attracts the territorial requirements in section 57.

[24] Sub-paragraph b. provides a special disapplication for core rules 5 and 6. The first of these is built on the conclusion that, if an unauthorised person can issue an advertisement without it requiring approval under the regulatory regime, then an authorised person ought to be able to do the same. It would be unfair to impose a burden on an authorised person in this respect simply because he happened to be authorised. The second limb frees from control under rules 5 and 6 advertisements issued by or governed by the rules of a designated investment exchange. This does not apply to the International Stock Exchange, but is in alignment with the exemption created for listing particulars and other documents required or permitted to be published by listing rules (see section 58(1)(d) of the Financial Services Act 1986). Also freed from control are advertisements subject to the takeover code, and scheme particulars, which are governed by the product regulation concerning regulated collective investment schemes. If, however, the scheme particulars themselves 'constitute' a direct offer advertisement, the two advertising core rules are reapplied.

[25] Paragraph c. deals with the reissue of advertisements, freeing reissue from control if, broadly speaking, there would not have been control in the first place for the original issue, or if, in the first place, it was properly controlled and passed the test of control. An advertisement cannot, however, without fresh scrutiny, be reissued to private customers if it was originally designed and intended only for non-private customers. The paragraph operates on the basis of a reasonable belief, so as not to penalise a firm which has such a belief about the circumstances of the previous issue by another person, even where that belief is actually mistaken.

[26] Paragraph (3) deals with the transitional application, and looks forward to subsequent commencement instruments to be made by the SIB.

[27] Paragraph (4) on interpretation is self-explanatory. The glossary referred to appears in annex 4.

NOTES

[1] For the definition of UCITS, see Chapter 3, note 7 (page 41 above).

PART C THE FINANCIAL SUPERVISION CORE RULES

CHAPTER 12

CORE RULES FOR FINANCIAL SUPERVISION

[1] There have been in operation since the Summer of 1990 five core rules relating to financial supervision. These rules are contained in the SIB's Financial Supervision Rules 1990, which were made on 21 June 1990, and came into force on 1 August 1990. Although a transitional provision has the effect that other provisions of those rules come into force on a date chosen by the firm or on 1 August 1991, that transitional provision does not apply to the five core rules.

[2] It will readily be seen from the core rules as set out (together) in annex 3 or (individually) below, that they are of a different character from those concerning the conduct of business. First, rules on financial supervision do not attract civil liability,[1] and, accordingly, are generally seen as a bilateral matter between the firm and the regulator, though one of major systemic and 'peer-group' concern to other firms. Secondly, the substance of the individual core rules is such as to refer in most if not all cases to rules or requirements laid down by the individual regulator. In this sense, therefore, they are more of a summary of the detailed ('third tier') rules relating to financial supervision than free-standing obligations of their own.

[3] While two of the five core rules (C and D) operate directly, rather than by reference to rules and requirements of the regulator, even these impose obligations which relate to other obligations to be found in the third tier, whether directly (as in the case of core rule C on internal controls and systems) or indirectly, through the core rules (as in the case of core rule D – *ad hoc* reporting).

Financial resources.

A. A firm must at all times have available the amount and type of financial resources required by the rules of its regulator.

Under core rule A, the firm's duty to have available the amount and type of financial resources required is a constant duty, that is 'at all times'. Experience with collapses of investment businesses over the last three to four years shows that it is indeed important that financial resources be constantly monitored by the firm, and any deficiency speedily rectified.

Records and reporting.

B. A firm must ensure that it maintains adequate accounting records and must prepare and submit such reports as are required by its regulator in a timely manner. A firm's records:

a. must be up to date and must disclose, with reasonable accuracy, at any time, the firm's financial position at that time;

b. must enable the firm to demonstrate its continuing compliance with its financial resources requirements, and

c. must provide the information:

i which the firm needs to prepare such financial statements and periodical reports as may be required by its regulator, and

ii which the firm's auditor (where the regulator requires one to be appointed) needs to form an opinion on any statements of the firm on which the auditor is required to report.

Under core rule B, the firm has to maintain adequate accounting records for the four purposes set out in a., b. and c.i and ii. Reports have also to be prepared and submitted to the regulator in a timely manner but only when required by the regulator either in lower level requirements or *ad hoc*.

[4] On the content and quality of records, paragraph a. requires the records to be up to date, and to disclose, with reasonable accuracy, at any time, the firm's financial position at that time. The expression 'up to date' does not necessarily mean 'on-line – real-time' recording, although this will be appropriate for some firms. On the other hand, records should not be allowed to slip too far into arrears. The records must be sufficient to disclose 'at any time' with reasonable accuracy the firm's financial position at that time. The inclusion of the words 'with reasonable accuracy' means that there is a margin of tolerance, and a set of records does not have to be exhaustively accurate at all times.

[5] The records must, under paragraph b., be maintained in such a way as to enable the firm to demonstrate continuing compliance with its financial resources requirements. This is perhaps a more exacting requirement than the one in a., in that the records needed to demonstrate continuing compliance will be more detailed and wide ranging than those required to show the firm's financial position.

[6] Requirement c.i stipulates that the firm's records must be those required to prepare such financial statements and periodical reports as the regulator may require. This means the periodic (monthly, quarterly, half-yearly and annual) reports received, depending on the category of authorisation. The sub-paragraph does not cover the *ad hoc* reporting required by core rule D, as reporting on those lines normally arises out of the routine recording and monitoring carried on by the firm.

[7] Sub-paragraph c.ii provides recording requirements to support the audit of the firm's accounts, and is often described as the requirement for 'an audit trail'.

Internal controls and systems.

> C. A firm must, for the purpose of its compliance with rules on financial supervision, ensure that its internal controls and systems are adequate for the size, nature and complexity of its activities.

Core rule C relates to internal controls and systems, and bears a striking similarity to a part of principle 9 (internal organisation). It spells out the concept of adequacy of internal controls and systems, by indicating that the adequacy must relate to the size, nature and complexity of the firm's activities. This allows for some flexibility in interpretation.

***Ad hoc* reporting.**

> D. A firm must notify its regulator immediately it becomes aware that it is in breach of, or that it expects shortly to be in breach of, the core rules on financial resources (A), records and reporting (B) or internal controls and systems (C).

Core rule D imposes a requirement on the firm to provide information to the regulator where there exists an actual breach or there is an anticipated breach of:

(a) the financial resources requirement itself;

(b) the requirement to keep adequate accounting records and to report adequately, or

(c) the requirement to have adequate internal controls and systems.

[8] Accordingly, if a firm expects to be unable to meet its financial resources requirement, it must tell the regulator in advance, so as to enable a kind of 'intensive care' to be applied during the anticipated period of difficulty. Equally, if there is a systems breakdown on records, or on a reporting requirement, or such a problem is envisaged, the firm must let the regulator know, and not simply hope

that the difficulty will not arise. Similarly, a systems breakdown, actual or anticipated, in terms of controls and/or systems triggers the need to involve the regulator.

Auditors.

E. A firm shall appoint an auditor where required to do so by its regulator. A firm shall make available to its auditor the information and explanations he needs to discharge his responsibilities as required by the firm's regulator.

Core rule E is in two parts. Under the first limb, the firm is required to appoint an auditor, where required to do so by the regulator: since most firms are UK limited companies, there is already a requirement under the Companies Acts to appoint an auditor, and so this part of the core rule applies only to those which are not already required to undergo statutory audit. In the second limb, the firm is required to make available to the auditor the information and explanations he needs to discharge his responsibilities. This part of the rule therefore is wider in impact, and applies to all firms with auditors, whether by virtue of the first half of the core rule or otherwise. The words 'as required by the firm's regulator' appear to relate to the discharge by the auditor of his responsibilities.

[9] **Application of financial supervision core rules.** The Financial Supervision Rules 1990 make specific provision for application, which differs in some respects from the application of the conduct of business core rules. In general:

(a) The financial supervision core rules apply to all directly regulated firms and to members of recognised self-regulating organisations. They have been applied to interim authorised firms by rules made in January 1991.

(b) These core rules do not, however, apply to any member of LAUTRO which is a regulated insurance company: nor do they apply to any member of IMRO or of LAUTRO which is a regulated friendly society. These firms are, of course, subject to separate and specific statutory regulatory arrangements including financial supervision.

(c) These rules do not apply where rules relating to financial supervision have been disapplied in their entirety in the case of a particular member of a self-regulating organisation (or an organisation regulated by SIB). An example of this is an overseas firm for which SIB and the SRO have entered into a lead regulation agreement for financial supervision with the 'home state' supervisor of the firm.

(d) In relation to directly regulated firms, there are further exceptions, for building societies, insurance companies and others that are subject to lead regulation of the kind just described.

NOTES

[1] See section 62(3) of the Financial Services Act 1986.

PART D

OTHER FORTHCOMING CORE REGULATIONS

[1] There are two other areas where the SIB has power to write designated provisions in the form of core regulations. The first of these relates to client money, and the second to unsolicited calls.

[2] The subject of client money is currently governed by the SIB's Financial Services (Clients' Money) Regulations 1987, and an equivalent set of regulations also made by the SIB were published for the three chartered accountancy bodies. Proposals relating to this subject were made[1] in the Spring of 1991. In view of the Companies Act 1989, part of all of such regulations would need to be 'designated', and thus regarded as core regulations, in their application to SROs. The SIB's power to write regulations direct in respect of persons certified by RPBs was left unaffected in the 1989 Act.

[3] As to unsolicited calls, proposals for a uniform new code on the subject loosely known as 'cold calling' were made by the SIB in October 1990. It has generally been thought convenient and simple to have a single code relating to the practice of cold calling, at any rate for members of SROs and directly regulated bodies, to whom alone the designated regulations could apply. The new uniform code is expected in the first half of 1991.

NOTES

[1] See the SIB's Consultative Paper No. 53 of April 1991: 'Proposals for amended Client Money Regulations'.

ANNEX 1

THE STATEMENTS OF PRINCIPLE

Introduction

[1] These principles are intended to form a universal statement of the standards expected. They apply directly to the conduct of investment business and financial standing of all authorised persons ('firms'), including members of recognised self-regulating organisations and firms certified by recognised professional bodies.

[2] The principles are not exhaustive of the standards expected. Conformity with the principles does not absolve a failure to observe other requirements, while the observance of other requirements does not necessarily amount to conformity with the principles.

[3] The principles do not give rise to actions for damages, but will be available for purposes of discipline and intervention.

[4] Where the principles refer to customers, they should be taken to refer also to clients and to potential customers, and where they refer to a firm's regulator, they mean SIB, or a self-regulating organisation or professional body which regulates the firm.

[5] Although the principles may be taken as expressing existing standards, they came into force formally, with additional sanctions resulting, on 30 April 1990.

1 Integrity

A firm should observe high standards of integrity and fair dealing.

2 Skill, Care and Diligence

A firm should act with due skill, care and diligence.

3 Market Practice

A firm should observe high standards of market conduct. It should also, to the extent endorsed for the purpose of this principle, comply with any code or standard as in force from time to time and as it applies to the firm either according to its terms or by rulings made under it.

4 Information about Customers

A firm should seek from customers it advises or for whom it exercises discretion any information about their circumstances and investment objectives which might reasonably be expected to be relevant in enabling it to fulfil its responsibilities to them.

5 Information for Customers

A firm should take reasonable steps to give a customer it advises, in a comprehensible and timely way, any information needed to enable him to make a balanced and informed decision. A firm should similarly be ready to provide a customer with a full and fair account of the fulfilment of its responsibilities to him.

6 Conflicts of Interest

A firm should either avoid any conflict of interest arising or, where conflicts arise, should ensure fair treatment to all its customers by disclosure, internal rules of confidentiality, declining to act, or otherwise. A firm should not unfairly place its interests above those of its customers and, where a properly informed customer would reasonably expect that the firm would place his interests above its own, the firm should live up to that expectation.

7 Customer Assets

Where a firm has control of or is otherwise responsible for assets belonging to a customer which it is required to safeguard, it should arrange proper protection for them, by way of segregation and identification of those assets or otherwise, in accordance with the responsibility it has accepted.

8 Financial Resources

A firm should ensure that it maintains adequate financial resources to meet its investment business commitments and to withstand the risks to which its business is subject.

9 Internal Organisation

A firm should organise and control its internal affairs in a responsible manner, keeping proper records, and where the firm employs staff or is responsible for the conduct of investment business by others, should have adequate arrangements to ensure that they are suitable, adequately trained and properly supervised and that it has well-defined compliance procedures.

10 Relations with regulators

A firm should deal with its regulator in an open and cooperative manner and keep the regulator promptly informed of anything concerning the firm which might reasonably be expected to be disclosed to it.

ANNEX 2

THE CORE CONDUCT OF BUSINESS RULES

Note: rules printed in italics apply only where a firm is providing investment services to a private customer.

INDEPENDENCE

1 Inducements

A firm must take reasonable steps to ensure that neither it nor any of its agents:

a. offers or gives, or

b. solicits or accepts,

either in the course of regulated business or otherwise any inducement which is likely significantly to conflict with any duties of the recipient (or the recipient's employer) owed to customers in connection with regulated business.

2 Material interest

Where a firm has a material interest in a transaction to be entered into with or for a customer or a relationship which gives rise to a conflict of interest in relation to such a transaction, the firm must not knowingly either advise, or deal in the exercise of discretion, in relation to that transaction unless it takes reasonable steps to ensure fair treatment for the customer.

3 Soft commission

A firm which deals for a customer on an advisory basis or in the exercise of discretion may not so deal through a broker pursuant to a soft commission agreement unless:

a. the only benefits to be provided under the agreement are goods or services which can reasonably be expected to assist in the provision of investment services to the firm's customers and which are in fact so used;

b. the broker has agreed to provide best execution to the customer;

c. the firm is satisfied on reasonable grounds that the terms of business and methods by which the relevant broking services will be supplied do not involve any potential for comparative price disadvantage to the customer;

d. in transactions in which the broker acts as principal, he is not remunerated by spread alone; and

e. adequate prior and periodic disclosure is made.

4 Polarisation

(1) A firm which advises a private customer on packaged products must either:

a. be a product company or its marketing group associate; or

b. do so as an independent intermediary.

(2) A firm which is a product company or its marketing group associate must not advise private customers to buy packaged products which are not those of the marketing group.

(3) A firm which acts as an independent intermediary in advising a private customer on packaged products must act as an independent intermediary whenever it advises private customers on packaged products in the course of regulated business.

(4) But where a firm acts as an investment manager for a customer, the core rule on polarisation does not prevent the firm from advising the customer on any packaged product.

ADVERTISING AND MARKETING

5 Issue and approval of advertisements

(1) Where a firm issues or approves an investment advertisement, it must:

a. apply appropriate expertise; and

b. be able to show that it believes on reasonable grounds that the advertisement is fair and not misleading.

(2) Where a firm issues or approves a specific investment advertisement it must ensure that the advertisement identifies it as issuer or approver, and also identifies its regulator.

(3) A firm must not approve a specific investment advertisement if it relates to units in an unregulated collective investment scheme.

(4) A firm must take reasonable steps to ensure that it does not issue or approve a direct offer advertisement for the sale of investments or the provision of investment services to a private customer unless the advertisement:

a. gives information about the investments or investment services, the terms of the offer, and the risks involved, which is adequate and fair having regard to the (UK or overseas) regulatory protections which apply and the market to which the advertisement is directed; and

b. offers derivatives or warrants only where the firm itself issues the advertisement and does so only to a customer for whom it believes on reasonable grounds the investment or investment services to be suitable.

6 Issue or approval of advertisements for an overseas person

A firm must not issue or approve a specific investment advertisement which is calculated to lead directly or indirectly to an overseas person carrying on investment business:

a. which is not regulated business; and

b. with or for a private customer who is in the United Kingdom;

unless both the advertisement contains the prescribed disclosure and the firm has no reason to doubt that the overseas person will deal with investors in the United Kingdom in an honest and reliable way.

7 Overseas business for UK private customers

(1) A firm must not carry on investment business:

a. which is not regulated business; and

b. with or for a private customer who is in the United Kingdom;

unless it has made the prescribed disclosure to the customer.

(2) A firm must not give an introduction or advice, or make arrangements, with a view to another person carrying on such business with or for such a customer, unless it has both made the prescribed disclosure and has no reason to doubt that the customer will be dealt with in an honest and reliable way.

8 Business conducted from an overseas place of business with overseas customers

If, in any communication made or advertisement issued to a private customer outside the United Kingdom in connection with investment business which is not regulated business, a firm indicates that it is an authorised person, it must also, and with equal prominence, make the prescribed disclosure.

9 Fair and clear communications

(1) A firm may make a communication with another person which is designed to promote the provision of investment services only if it can show that it believes on reasonable grounds that the communication is fair and not misleading.

(2) A firm must take reasonable steps to ensure that any agreement, written communication, notification or information which it gives or sends to a private customer to whom it provides investment services is presented fairly and clearly.

10 Customers' understanding

A firm must not recommend a transaction to a private customer, or act as a discretionary manager for him, unless it has taken reasonable steps to enable him to understand the nature of the risks involved.

11 Information about the firm

(1) A firm must take reasonable steps to ensure that a private customer to whom it provides investment services is given adequate information about its identity and business address, the identity and status with the firm of employees and other relevant agents with whom the customer has contact and the identity of the firm's regulator.

(2) Unless a firm is acting as an investment manager, it must take reasonable steps to ensure that a private customer it advises to buy a packaged product is also given adequate information about the firm's polarisation status, the buying process and any limits on the packaged products on which it can advise.

12 Information about packaged products

(1) Before or when making a personal recommendation to a private customer to buy a packaged product, a firm must give him information about the product which is adequate to enable him to make an informed investment decision.

(2) Before or as soon as practicable after a private customer buys a packaged product in a transaction recommended, effected or arranged

by a firm, the firm must provide him with appropriate written product particulars unless:

a. the firm buys the packaged product as a discretionary investment manager; or

b. the transaction is effected or arranged on an execution-only basis.

13 Appointed representatives

(1) A firm must satisfy itself on reasonable grounds and on a continuing basis that any appointed representative it appoints is fit and proper to act for it in that capacity.

(2) A firm must also satisfy itself on reasonable grounds and on a continuing basis that it has adequate resources to monitor and enforce compliance by its appointed representatives with high standards of business conduct.

(3) A firm must ensure that any of its appointed representatives carries on regulated business for which the firm has accepted responsibility only:

a. in circumstances where the representative does not carry on (or purport to carry on) in the United Kingdom any investment business for which the representative is not an authorised or exempted person; and

b. in a way which ensures that the business for which the firm has accepted responsibility is, and is held out as being, clearly distinct from any financial business which the representative carries on which is not investment business, unless that other financial business is covered by authorisation under an enactment as a bank or building society;

but a firm does not break this requirement if it can show it has taken reasonable steps to comply with it.

(4) Subject to any exceptions contained in the rules of an SRO of which it is a member, a firm must ensure that its employment of any of its appointed representatives can be terminated only with the authority of its regulator.

CUSTOMER RELATIONS

14 Customer agreements

(1) Where a firm provides investment services to a private customer (other than an indirect customer) on written contractual terms, the agreement must set out in adequate detail the basis on which those services are provided.

(2) Where a firm provides to a private customer (other than an indirect customer) investment services involving:

a. contingent liability transactions; or

b. the discretionary management of the customer's assets;

it must do so under a two way customer agreement unless the customer is ordinarily resident outside the United Kingdom and the firm believes on reasonable grounds that he does not wish a two way agreement to be used.

15 Customers' rights

(1) A firm must not, in any written communication or agreement, seek to exclude or restrict any duty or liability to a customer which it has under the Act, or under the regulatory system.

(2) Similarly, unless it is reasonable to do so in the circumstances, a firm must not, in any written communication or agreement, seek to exclude or restrict:

a. any other duty to act with skill, care and diligence which is owed to a private customer in connection with the provision to him of investment services in the course of regulated business; or

b. any liability owed to a private customer in connection with regulated business for failure to exercise the degree of skill, care and diligence which may reasonably be expected of it in the provision of investment services in the course of that business.

(3) A firm must not seek unreasonably to rely on any provision seeking to exclude or restrict any such duty or liability.

16 Suitability

(1) A firm must take reasonable steps to ensure that it does not in the course of regulated business or associated business:

a. make any personal recommendation to a private customer of an investment or investment agreement; or

b. effect or arrange a discretionary transaction with or for a private customer or, subject to any exceptions contained in the rules of an SRO of which the firm is a member, any other customer;

unless the recommendation or transaction is suitable for him having regard to the facts disclosed by that customer and other relevant facts about the customer of which the firm is, or reasonably should be, aware.

(2) But where, with the agreement of the customer, a firm has pooled his funds with those of others with a view to taking common management decisions, the firm must instead take reasonable steps to ensure that the transaction is suitable for the fund, having regard to the stated investment objectives of the fund.

17 Standards of advice on packaged products

(1) A firm which advises private customers to buy packaged products must take reasonable steps to inform itself and relevant agents:

a. where the firm is a product company or its marketing group associate, about packaged products available from the marketing group; or

b. where the firm is an independent intermediary, about packaged products which are generally available on the market and on which it can advise.

(2) Where a firm is a product company or its marketing group associate, it must not advise a private customer to buy a packaged product, or buy a packaged product for him in the exercise of discretion, if it is aware of a packaged product of the marketing group which would better meet his needs.

(3) *Where a firm is acting as an independent intermediary, it must not advise a private customer to buy a packaged product, or buy a packaged product for him in the exercise of discretion, if it is aware of a generally available packaged product which would better meet his needs.*

(4) *Where a firm is a product company or its marketing group associate and is acting as an investment manager, it must not advise a private customer to buy a packaged product of a product company outside the marketing group, or buy such a product for him in the exercise of discretion, if it is, or reasonably should be, aware of a generally available packaged product which would better meet his needs.*

(5) *Where a firm is acting for a private customer as an independent intermediary but not as an investment manager, it must not advise him to buy a packaged product from its extended group if it is aware of a generally available packaged product which is not a product of the extended group and which would meet his needs as well as the extended group product.*

(6) *In assessing the merits of a packaged product to be held as the plan investment of a personal equity plan, a firm must take into account the characteristics (including charging arrangements) of the plan, as well as those of the product.*

18 Charges and other remuneration

(1) *The amount of a firm's charges to a private customer for the provision of investment services to him must not be unreasonable in the circumstances.*

(2) *Subject to any exceptions contained in the rules of an SRO of which it is a member, before a firm provides investment services to a private customer (other than an indirect customer), it must disclose to him the basis or amount of its charges for the provision of those services and the nature or amount of any other remuneration receivable by it (or, to its knowledge, by its associate) and attributable to them.*

19 Confirmations and periodic information

(1) Subject to any exceptions contained in the rules of an SRO of which it is a member, a firm which effects a sale or purchase of an investment

(other than a life policy) with or for a customer must ensure that he is sent with due despatch a note containing the essential details of the transaction.

(2) Subject to any exceptions contained in the rules of an SRO of which it is a member, a firm which acts as an investment manager for a customer must ensure that he is sent at suitable intervals a report stating the value of the portfolio or account at the beginning and end of the period, its composition at the end, and, in the case of a discretionary portfolio or account, changes in its composition between those dates.

DEALING FOR CUSTOMERS

20 Customer order priority

A firm should deal with customer and own account orders fairly and in due turn.

21 Timely execution

(1) Once a firm has agreed or decided in its discretion to effect or arrange a current customer order, it must effect or arrange the execution of the order as soon as reasonably practicable in the circumstances.

(2) But the core rule on timely execution does not preclude a firm from postponing execution of an order where it believes on reasonable grounds that this is in the best interests of the customer.

22 Best execution

(1) Where a firm deals with or for a private customer, it must provide best execution.

(2) A firm must also provide best execution where it fulfils an order from a non-private customer.

(3) A firm may rely on another person who executes the transaction to provide best execution, but only if it believes on reasonable grounds that he will do so.

(4) For the purposes of the core rule on best execution, a firm provides best execution if:

a. it takes reasonable care to ascertain the price which is the best available for the customer in the relevant market at the time for transactions of the kind and size concerned; and

b. unless the circumstances require it to do otherwise in the interests of the customer, it deals at a price which is no less advantageous to him;

and in applying the core rule on best execution, a firm should leave out of account any charges disclosed to the customer which it or its agent would make.

(5) The core rule on best execution does not require a firm to provide best execution on a purchase of a life policy or on a purchase from the operator of a regulated collective investment scheme of units in the scheme.

23 Timely allocation

A firm must ensure that a transaction it executes is promptly allocated.

24 Fair allocation

Where a firm has aggregated an order for a customer transaction with an order for an own account transaction, or with another order for a customer transaction, then in the subsequent allocation:

a. it must not give unfair preference to itself or to any of those for whom it dealt; and

b. if all cannot be satisfied, it must give priority to satisfying orders for customer transactions unless it believes on reasonable grounds that, without its own participation, it would not have been able to effect those orders either on such favourable terms or at all.

25 Dealing ahead of publications

Subject to any exceptions contained in the rules of an SRO of which it is a member, where a firm or its associate intends to publish to customers a recommendation or a piece of research or analysis, it must not knowingly effect an own account transaction in the investment concerned or any related investment until the customers for whom the publication was principally intended have had (or are likely to have had) a reasonable opportunity to react to it.

26 Churning and switching

(1) A firm must not:

a. make a personal recommendation to a private customer to deal; or

b. deal or arrange a deal in the exercise of discretion for any customer;

if the dealing would reasonably be regarded as too frequent in the circumstances.

(2) A firm must not:

a. make a personal recommendation to a private customer to switch within a packaged product or between packaged products; or

b. effect such a switch in the exercise of discretion for a private customer;

unless it believes on reasonable grounds that the switch is justified from the customer's viewpoint.

27 Certain derivatives transactions to be on exchange

A firm must not effect, arrange or recommend a contingent liability transaction with, for or to a private customer unless:

a. the transaction is made on a recognised or designated investment exchange; or

b. the firm believes on reasonable grounds that the purpose of the transaction is to hedge against currency risk involved in a position which the customer holds.

MARKET INTEGRITY

28 Insider dealing

(1) A firm must not effect (either in the United Kingdom or elsewhere) an own account transaction when it knows of circumstances which mean that it, its associate, or an employee of either, is prohibited from effecting that transaction by the statutory restrictions on insider dealing.

(2) A firm must use its best endeavours to ensure that it does not knowingly effect (either in the course of regulated business or otherwise) a transaction for a customer it knows is so prohibited.

(3) But the core rule on insider dealing does not apply where:

a. the prohibition applies only because of knowledge of the firm's own intentions;

b. the firm is a recognised market maker with obligations to deal in the investment; or

c. the firm is a trustee or personal representative who acts on the advice of a third party appearing to be an appropriate adviser who is not so prohibited.

29 Stabilisation of securities

Where a firm takes action (either in the course of regulated business or otherwise) for the purpose of stabilising the price of securities, it must comply with any applicable provisions of the statutory stabilisation rules.

30 Off-exchange market makers

Where a firm sells to a private customer any securities which are not quoted on a recognised or designated investment exchange, whilst giving the customer the impression that the firm is a market maker in the investment concerned, it must:

a. give notice to the customer that it is required to ensure that a reasonable price for repurchase of the investment is available to him for a specified period which must not be less than three months after the date the notice is given; and

b. ensure that such a price is available to him for that specified period.

31 Reportable transactions

Unless otherwise provided by the rules of an SRO of which it is a member, a firm must make available to its regulator details about transactions (including own account transactions) in securities which it effects other than on a recognised investment exchange.

ADMINISTRATION

32 Safeguarding of customer investments

A firm which has custody of a customer's investments in connection with or with a view to regulated business must, subject to any exceptions contained in the rules of an SRO of which it is a member:

a. keep safe, or arrange for the safekeeping of, any documents of title relating to them;

b. ensure that any registrable investments which it buys or holds for a customer in the course of regulated business are properly registered in his name or, with the consent of the customer, in the name of an eligible nominee; and

c. where title to investments is recorded electronically, ensure that customer entitlements are separately identifiable from those of the firm in the records of the person maintaining records of entitlement.

33 Scope of business

A firm must maintain a business profile describing the kind of investment business it carries on in the United Kingdom and may carry on (and hold itself out as carrying on) investment business in the United Kingdom of that kind only.

34 Compliance

(1) A firm must take reasonable steps, including the establishment and maintenance of procedures, to ensure that its officers and employees and officers and employees of its appointed representatives act in conformity with:

a. their own and their employer's relevant responsibilities under the regulatory system;

b. where relevant, the requirements of the statutory restrictions on insider dealing; and

c. appropriate arrangements on propriety in personal dealings.

(2) A firm must take reasonable steps, including the establishment and maintenance of procedures, to ensure that sufficient information is recorded and retained about its regulated business and compliance with the regulatory system.

(3) Records required to be maintained by the regulatory system may be inspected by a person appointed for the purpose by the firm's regulator.

35 Complaints

(1) A firm must have procedures to ensure:

a. the proper handling of complaints from customers relevant to its compliance with the regulatory system;

b. that any appropriate remedial action on those complaints is promptly taken; and

c. where the complaint is not promptly remedied, that the customer is advised of any further avenue for complaint available to him under the regulatory system.

(2) A firm must cooperate with a person appointed by its regulator to investigate complaints.

36 Chinese walls

(1) Where a firm maintains an established arrangement which requires information obtained by the firm in the course of carrying on one part of its business of any kind to be withheld in certain circumstances from persons with whom it deals in the course of carrying on another part of its business of any kind, then in those circumstances:

a. that information may be so withheld; and

b. for that purpose, persons employed in the first part may withhold information from those employed in the second;

but only to the extent that the business of one of those parts involves investment business or associated business.

(2) Information may also be withheld where this is required by an established arrangement between different parts of the business (of any kind) of a group, but this provision does not affect any requirement to transmit information which may arise apart from the Core Conduct of Business Rules.

(3) Where the Core Conduct of Business Rules apply only if a firm acts with knowledge, the firm is not for the purposes of the Core Conduct of Business Rules to be taken to act with knowledge if none of the relevant individuals involved on behalf of the firm acts with knowledge.

(4) In addition, in order to avoid the attribution of information held within a firm to that firm for the purposes of section 47 of the Act, the effect of section 48(6) of the Act is that nothing done in conformity with paragraph (1) of the core rule on Chinese walls is to be regarded as a contravention of section 47 of the Act.

37 Cessation of business

(1) Where a firm or its appointed representative decides to withdraw from providing any investment or related custodian services to private customers, the firm must ensure that any such business which is outstanding is properly completed or is transferred to another firm.

(2) *Where the interests of private customers of a firm would be significantly affected by the death or incapacity of an individual within the firm, the firm must make arrangements to protect the interests of those customers in that event.*

GENERAL

38 Reliance on others

(1) A person is to be taken to act in conformity with the Core Conduct of Business Rules to the extent that:

a. the relevant regulator has issued formal guidance on compliance with them; and

b. in reliance on standards set in that guidance, the person concerned believes on reasonable grounds that he is acting in conformity with the rules.

(2) A person is to be taken to act in conformity with any of the Core Conduct of Business Rules as to information, to the extent that he can show that he reasonably relied on information provided to him in writing by a third party whom he believed on reasonable grounds to be independent and competent to provide the information.

(3) Any communication required under the Core Conduct of Business Rules to be sent to a customer may be sent to the order of the customer, so long as the recipient is independent of the firm; and there is no need for a firm to send a communication itself where it believes on reasonable grounds that this has been or will be supplied direct by another person.

39 Classes of customer

(1) *The Core Conduct of Business Rules apply subject to any exceptions contained in the rules of an SRO of which the firm is a member which enable it to treat a customer who would otherwise be a private customer as a non-private customer for the purposes of the Core Conduct of Business Rules if:*

a. it can show that it believes on reasonable grounds that the customer has sufficient experience and understanding to waive the protections provided for private customers;

b. it has given a clear written warning to the customer of the protections under the regulatory system which he will lose; and

c. the customer has given his written consent after a proper opportunity to consider that warning.

(2) But SRO rules need not require written consent where the customer is ordinarily resident outside the United Kingdom and is reasonably believed not to wish to consent in writing.

40 Application of the Core Conduct of Business Rules

(1) **Business**

a. The general application of the Core Conduct of Business Rules is that, as far as they relate to business, they relate to business which is regulated business, and accordingly, where a rule relating to business applies only in particular circumstances, the rule applies only if those circumstances apply in the course of regulated business.

b. To the extent indicated, the Core Conduct of Business Rules also apply to the carrying on (whether in the UK or elsewhere) of other business if that other business is investment business, associated business or business which is held out as being for the purposes of investment.

c. The Core Conduct of Business Rules do not apply to authorised persons to the extent that they are acting as authorised persons certified by recognised professional bodies (since these persons are subject to regulation by those bodies) or to the extent that they are acting as exempted persons.

d. The Core Conduct of Business Rules are limited in their application to regulated insurance companies (by paragraph 4 of Schedule 10 to the Act), to regulated friendly societies (by paragraph 14 of Schedule 11 to the Act) and to certain UCITS operators and trustees (by section 86(7) of the Act).

e. The Core Conduct of Business Rules apply to an oil market participant subject to exceptions contained in the rules of an SRO of which the firm is a member.

f. Where the firm is:

(i) a journalist, broadcaster, author or publisher;

(ii) whose only investment business is the provision of investment advice;

the Core Conduct of Business Rules apply subject to exceptions contained in the rules of an SRO of which the firm is a member.

(2) **Advertisements**

a. Where the Core Conduct of Business Rules govern the issue or approval of an investment advertisement then, except to the extent indicated, they govern issue of an investment advertisement in the United Kingdom and approval (whether in the United Kingdom or elsewhere) of an investment advertisement for issue in the United Kingdom.

b. The Core Conduct of Business Rules on issue and approval of advertisements and on issue or approval of advertisements for an overseas person do not apply:

(i) to the issue by an authorised person of an exempt advertisement; or

(ii) to the issue or approval of a DIE advertisement, a takeover advertisement, or (unless they constitute a direct offer advertisement) scheme particulars.

c. The Core Conduct of Business Rules do not apply to the reissue of an investment advertisement which has been prepared and issued by another person and which the firm believes on reasonable grounds:

(i) is an exempt advertisement, a DIE advertisement, a takeover advertisement, or (unless they constitute a direct offer advertisement) scheme particulars; or

(ii) is already issued or approved by an authorised person and is issued to a market for which it was intended at the time of its issue or approval by the authorised person.

(3) **Time**

The application of the Core Conduct of Business Rules as to time is that they apply to a firm from the date specified for firms of the relevant class in a separate commencement instrument made by the Board (subject to any transitional provisions contained in that instrument).

(4) **Interpretation**

a. The Financial Services Glossary 1991 applies, unless the context otherwise requires, for the interpretation of the Core Conduct of Business Rules.

b. Any other expressions defined for the purposes of the Act, or in the Interpretation Act 1978, have the same meanings in the Core Conduct of Business Rules.

c. These rules may be cited as the Core Conduct of Business Rules. They are made under section 48 of and, for friendly societies, paragraph 14 of Schedule 11 to, the Act. They are designated so as to apply directly to members of recognised self-regulating organisations under section 63A of and, for friendly societies, paragraph 22B of Schedule 11 to, the Act.

ANNEX 3

THE FINANCIAL SUPERVISION CORE RULES

A. **Financial resources.** A firm must at all times have available the amount and type of financial resources required by the rules of its regulator.

B. **Records and reporting.** A firm must ensure that it maintains adequate accounting records and must prepare and submit such reports as are required by its regulator in a timely manner. A firm's records:

a. must be up to date and must disclose, with reasonable accuracy, at any time, the firm's financial position at that time;

b. must enable the firm to demonstrate its continuing compliance with its financial resources requirements, and

c. must provide the information:

(i) which the firm needs to prepare such financial statements and periodical reports as may be required by its regulator, and

(ii) which the firm's auditor (where the regulator requires one to be appointed) needs to form an opinion on any statements of the firm on which the auditor is required to report.

C. **Internal controls and systems.** A firm must, for the purpose of its compliance with rules on financial supervision, ensure that its internal controls and systems are adequate for the size, nature and complexity of its activities.

D. ***Ad hoc* reporting.** A firm must notify its regulator immediately it becomes aware that it is in breach of, or that it expects shortly to be in breach of, the core rules on financial resources (A), records and reporting (B) or internal controls and systems (C).

E. **Auditors.** A firm shall appoint an auditor where required to do so by its regulator. A firm shall make available to its auditor the information and explanations he needs to discharge his responsibilities as required by the firm's regulator.

ANNEX 4

THE FINANCIAL SERVICES GLOSSARY 1991

Introduction

This Glossary is designed to establish standard meanings for expressions used in rules or regulations made by the Board under the Financial Services Act 1986.

Where these standard meanings are to apply, this will be stated in the rules or regulations concerned.

This text shows the meanings established as at 28 January 1991.

Glossary

1 The following expressions have the following meanings unless the context otherwise requires:

the **Act** means the Financial Services Act 1986;

agent, in relation to a person, means any person (including an employee) who acts on that person's behalf;

ancillary, in relation to an investment, means any right to or interest in that investment which falls within paragraph 11 of Schedule 1 to the Act;

approve, in relation to an investment advertisement, means approve for the purposes of section 57 of the Act;

associate, in relation to a person, means:

(a) an undertaking in the same group as that person;

(b) an appointed representative of the first person or of any undertaking in the same group; and

(c) any other person whose business or domestic relationship with the first person or its associate might reasonably be expected to give rise to a community of interest between them which may involve a conflict of interest in dealings with third parties;

associated business means business which is carried on in connection with investment business;

broker includes broker-dealer;

buy has the meaning given by paragraph 28 of Schedule 1 to the Act;

the Board means the Securities and Investments Board;

certificates representing securities means investments falling within paragraph 5 of Schedule 1 to the Act;

charges means any charges made to a customer in connection with investment services, including any mark-up or mark-down from the price at which best execution would be achieved;

contingent liability transaction means a derivatives transaction under the terms of which the customer will or may be liable to make further payments (other than charges, and whether or not secured by margin) when the transaction falls to be completed or upon the earlier closing out of his position;

contract for differences means an investment falling within paragraph 9 of Schedule 1 to the Act;

current customer order includes both a customer order for immediate execution and, once the condition is fulfilled, a customer order which is only to be executed on fulfilment of a condition;

customer does not include a market counterparty or a trust beneficiary but includes:

(a) a potential customer;

(b) an indirect customer; and

(c) a customer of an appointed representative of a firm with or for whom the representative acts in the course of business for which the firm has accepted responsibility;

customer transaction does not include an own account transaction;

debenture means an investment falling within paragraph 2 of Schedule 1 to the Act;

derivatives means options, futures and contracts for differences;

designated investment exchange means any investment exchange which is designated by the Board as a designated investment exchange for the purposes of the Financial Services (Conduct of Business) Rules 1990 or the Core Conduct of Business Rules;

DIE advertisement means an advertisement:

(a) issued by a designated investment exchange; or

(b) required or permitted to be published by the rules of a designated investment exchange;

direct offer advertisement means a specific investment advertisement (including a pre-printed or off-the-screen advertisement) which:

(a) contains:

(i) an offer by the firm or another offeror to enter into an investment agreement with anyone who responds to the advertisement; or

(ii) an invitation to anyone to respond to the advertisement by making an offer to the firm or another offeree to enter into an investment agreement; and

(b) specifies the manner or indicates a form in which any response is to be made (for example by providing a tear-off slip);

disclosable commission means commission which the regulatory system requires to be disclosed to a customer;

eligible nominee means:

(a) an individual chosen by the customer who is not known by the firm to be an associate of the firm;

(b) a corporate nominee with no other business; or

(c) an institution authorised under the Banking Act 1987;

exception, in relation to the rules of an SRO, means any provision made after 1 February 1991 which expressly disapplies or qualifies any particular Core Conduct of Business Rule in relation to a specific description of member firms, customers, transactions or circumstances;

exempt advertisement means an investment advertisement which can lawfully be issued in the United Kingdom by a person who is not an authorised person without approval of its contents by an authorised person;

extended group means the extended group consisting of the members of a group of undertakings and the marketing group associates of any of them;

financial business means business which is, or is held out as being, primarily for the purposes of investment;

firm means an authorised person under the Act;

formal guidance means guidance which is intended to have continuing effect and is issued:

(a) generally or to a class of persons; and

(b) in writing or other legible form;

future means an investment falling within paragraph 8 of Schedule 1 to the Act;

government and public securities means investments falling within paragraph 3 of Schedule 1 to the Act;

group, except in relation to a marketing group, has the meaning given by paragraph 30 of Schedule 1 to the Act;

indirect customer means, where a customer is known to be acting as agent, an identified principal who would be a customer if he were dealt with direct;

inducement does not include:

(a) disclosable commission; or

(b) goods or services which can reasonably be expected to assist in the provision of investment services to customers and which are provided or to be provided under a soft commission agreement;

investment manager means a person who, acting only on behalf of a customer, either:

(a) manages an account or portfolio in the exercise of discretion; or

(b) has accepted responsibility on a continuing basis for advising on the composition of the account or portfolio;

investment services means activities undertaken in the course of carrying on investment business;

investment trust means a closed-ended company which is listed in the United Kingdom or another member State and:

(a) is approved by the Inland Revenue under section 842 of the Income and Corporation Taxes Act 1988 (or, in the case of a newly formed company has declared its intention to conduct its affairs so as to obtain approval); or

(b) is resident in another member State and would qualify for approval if resident and listed in the United Kingdom;

investment trust savings scheme means a dealing service dedicated to the securities of a particular investment trust or of investment trusts within a particular marketing group (and references to an investment trust savings scheme include references to securities to be acquired through that scheme);

issue includes cause to be issued;

life policy means an investment falling within paragraph 10 of Schedule 1 to the Act;

market counterparty means a person dealing with the firm:

(a) as principal or as agent for an unidentified principal; and

(b) in the course of investment business of the same description as that in the course of which the firm acts;

marketing group means a group of persons who:

(a) are allied together (either formally or informally) for purposes of marketing packaged products of the group; and

(b) each of whom, if it holds itself out in the United Kingdom as marketing any packaged products to private investors, does so only as an investment manager or in relation to those of the marketing group;

marketing group associate, in relation to a person in a marketing group, means any other person which is a member of that marketing group;

market maker, in relation to an investment of any description, means a person who (otherwise than in his capacity as the operator of a regulated collective investment scheme) holds himself out as able and willing to enter into transactions of sale and purchase in investments of that description at prices determined by him generally and continuously rather than in respect of each particular transaction;

material interest, in relation to a transaction, does not include:

(a) disclosable commission on the transaction; or

(b) goods or services which can reasonably be expected to assist in the provision of investment services to customers and which are provided or to be provided under a soft commission agreement;

non-private customer means a customer who is not a private customer;

oil market participant has the same meaning as in the Financial Services (Conduct of Business) Rules 1990;

on exchange, in relation to a transaction, means that the transaction is effected:

(a) on the exchange;

(b) under the rules of the exchange; or

(c) as a transaction which is both matched and identified as matched with an on exchange transaction;

option means an investment falling within paragraph 7 of Schedule 1 to the Act;

order, in relation to an order from a customer, means:

(a) an order to a firm from the customer to effect a transaction as agent;

(b) any other order to a firm from the customer to effect a transaction in circumstances giving rise to similar duties as those arising on an order to effect a transaction as agent;

(c) a decision by a firm in the exercise of discretion for the customer;

ordinary business investor means:

(a) a government, local authority or public authority within the meaning of Schedule 1 to the Act;

(b) a company or partnership which satisfies any of the following size requirements:

(i) that it is a body corporate which has more than 20 members (or is the subsidiary of a company which has more than 20 members) and it (or any of its holding companies or subsidiaries) has a called up share capital or net assets of £500,000 or more;

(ii) that it is a body corporate and it (or any of its holding companies or subsidiaries) has a called up share capital or net assets of £5 million or more; or

(iii) if it is not a body corporate, it has net assets of £5 million or more; or

(c) a trustee of a trust which satisfies either of the following size requirements:

(i) that the aggregate value of the cash and investments which form part of the trust's assets (before deducting the amount of its liabilities) is £10 million or more; or

(ii) that that aggregate value has been £10 million or more at any time during the previous two years;

overseas person means a person who carries on investment business but who does not do so from a permanent place of business maintained by him in the United Kingdom;

own account transaction means a transaction:

(a) effected or arranged by the firm in the course of carrying on either investment business or associated business; and

(b) on its own account or on the account of an associate acting on its own account;

packaged product means a life policy, a unit in a regulated collective investment scheme, or an investment trust savings scheme;

prescribed disclosure means a written statement which must make clear:

(a) that all or most of the protections provided by the UK regulatory system do not apply; and

(b) where the business is excluded from the Investors Compensation Scheme by its territorial scope (or would be so excluded if the person carrying it on were a participant firm), a statement that compensation under that scheme will not be available;

and which may also indicate the protections or compensation available under another system of regulation;

Principles means the Statements of Principle made by the Board on 15 March 1990;

private customer means:

(a) a customer who is an individual and who is not acting in the course of carrying on investment business; or

(b) unless he is reasonably believed to be an ordinary business investor, a customer who is a small business investor;

product company means:

(a) in relation to a life policy, the life office by which that policy is issued;

(b) in relation to units in a regulated collective investment scheme, the operator of that scheme;

(c) in relation to an investment trust savings scheme, the operator of that scheme;

recognised market maker means a person (whether an individual, partnership or company) who:

(a) holds himself out at all normal times in compliance with the rules of a recognised investment exchange as willing to buy and sell securities at prices specified by him; and

(b) is recognised as doing so by that recognised investment exchange;

regulated business means investment business which is:

(a) business carried on from a permanent place of business maintained by a firm (or its appointed representative) in the United Kingdom; and

(b) other business carried on with or for customers in the United Kingdom, unless that business is:

(i) business carried on from an office of a firm outside the United Kingdom which would not be treated as carried on in the United Kingdom if that office were a separate person; or

(ii) business of an appointed representative of the firm which is not carried on in the United Kingdom;

regulated collective investment scheme means an authorised unit trust scheme or a recognised scheme;

regulated friendly society has the meaning given by paragraph 1 of Schedule 11 to the Act;

regulated insurance company means an insurance company:

(a) to which Part II of the Insurance Companies Act 1982 applies; or

(b) which is an authorised person by virtue of section 31 of the Act;

regulated life office means a regulated insurance company or a regulated friendly society;

regulator, in relation to a firm, means:

(a) where the firm is a member of an SRO, that SRO;

(b) where the firm is certified by a recognised professional body, that body; and

(c) otherwise, the Board;

regulatory system means the arrangements for regulating a firm under the Act including the Principles, the Core Conduct of Business Rules and the rules of its regulator;

sale has the meaning given by paragraph 28 of Schedule 1 to the Act;

scheme particulars means a document containing information about a regulated collective investment scheme and subject to requirements as to the content of scheme particulars made either:

(a) under the Act; or

(b) in the case of a scheme recognised under section 86 of the Act, by the certifying member State;

securities means shares, debentures, government and public securities, warrants and certificates representing securities;

share means an investment falling within paragraph 1 of Schedule 1 to the Act;

small business investor means:

(a) a company or partnership; or

(b) a trustee acting for a trust;

which does not satisfy a size requirement enabling the company, partnership or trustee to be treated as an ordinary business investor;

soft commission agreement means any agreement, whether oral or written, under which a firm which deals in securities on an advisory basis or in the exercise of discretion receives goods or services in return for an assurance that not less than a certain amount of such business will be put through or in the way of another person;

specific investment advertisement means an investment advertisement which identifies and promotes a particular investment or particular investment services;

SRO means a recognised self-regulating organisation;

statutory restrictions on insider dealing means the Company Securities (Insider Dealing) Act 1985;

statutory stabilisation rules means Part 10 of the Financial Services (Conduct of Business) Rules 1990;

takeover advertisement means an advertisement to which the Takeover Code applies (or would apply but for any exemption granted by the Panel on Takeovers and Mergers);

Takeover Code means the City Code on Takeovers and Mergers and the Rules Governing Substantial Acquisitions of Shares published by the Panel on Takeovers and Mergers;

trust beneficiary means a beneficiary under a trust (not being the settlor) who benefits from the performance by a firm as trustee of investment services relating to the management of the trust assets;

two-way customer agreement means an agreement in written form to which the customer has signified his assent in writing in circumstances where the firm is satisfied that the customer has had a proper opportunity to consider its terms; and

warrant means an investment falling within paragraph 4 of Schedule 1 to the Act.

2 Neither a soft commission agreement, nor an arrangement for the payment of disclosable commission, is to be taken for the purposes of the core rule on material interest as a relationship which gives rise to a conflict of interest in relation to transactions effected under the agreement or arrangement.

3 References to an investment include an ancillary on that investment.

4 Any expression which is related to any expression defined in this Glossary is to be construed accordingly.

ANNEX 5

RESOLUTION OF THE INTERNATIONAL ORGANISATION OF SECURITIES COMMISSIONS

INTERNATIONAL CONDUCT OF BUSINESS PRINCIPLES

(as published in 'IOSCO News' January 1991, Vol 12, No I, pp 9-11)

The Presidents' Committee approved the Report on International Conduct of Business Principles and directed that the report be distributed to all members of IOSCO.

Furthermore, the Presidents' Committee has called on all members of IOSCO to recognise the following set of international conduct of business principles as expressing basic standards of business conduct for financial firms in their activities on the domestic as well as the international level.

This recognition will commit IOSCO members to implement the principles through their regulatory structures and effective supervisory arrangements, and to try to promote the principles throughout their own countries. Each member can decide whether to implement them in the form stated by IOSCO or to reflect them in its principles, adapted to local circumstances.

These principles are:

1 HONESTY AND FAIRNESS

In conducting its business activities, a firm should act honestly and fairly in the best interests of its customers and the integrity of the market.

Comment:

This principle includes any obligation to avoid misleading and deceptive acts or representations.

2 DILIGENCE

In conducting its business activities, a firm should act with due skill, care and diligence, in the best interests of its customers and the integrity of the market.

Comment:

This principle includes any duty of best execution.

3 CAPABILITIES

A firm should have and employ effectively the resources and procedures which are needed for the proper performance of its business activities.

Comment:

This principle includes any obligation for the firm to have and implement effectively rules and internal procedures for its employees and representatives to make sure that they comply with these principles, including staff dealing rules.

4 INFORMATION ABOUT CUSTOMERS

A firm should seek from its customers information about their financial situation, investment experience and investment objectives relevant to the services to be provided.

Comment:

This principle includes any obligation to 'know one's customer'.

This principle is a necessary element in enabling the firm to fulfil any suitability requirements.

5 INFORMATION FOR CUSTOMERS

A firm should make adequate disclosure of relevant material information in its dealings with its customers.

Comment:

This principle includes any obligation of the firm:

(a) to acquire and to provide information, including information about risks, needed by the customer to make informed investment decisions;

(b) to provide timely and accurate reports to the customers about business undertaken for or with the customer.

6 CONFLICTS OF INTEREST

A firm should try to avoid conflicts of interest, and when they cannot be avoided, should ensure that its customers are fairly treated.

Comment:

This principle recognises that conflicts of interest may be managed, and that proper management to ensure fair treatment of customers may require disclosure, internal rules or confidentiality, or other appropriate methods or combinations of methods.

7 COMPLIANCE

A firm should comply with all regulatory requirements applicable to the conduct of its business activities so as to promote the best interests of customers and the integrity of the market.

The comments associated with the principles provide illustrations of some rules or obligations which might fall within the boundaries of individual principles, and may assist IOSCO members in implementing the principles. Moreover, the IOSCO Report on International Conduct of Business Principles (July 1990) may provide additional guidance to members in implementing the principles.

The members were also asked to advise the Secretary General of their recognition of the principles and on how and when they will implement them, in the event that such principles have not already been implemented in their jurisdiction.

The Secretary General will make a report at the next Annual Conference concerning the degree of implementation of the principles.

INDEX

Index

Index